BASICS OF DIGITIZATION

BASICS OF DIGITIZATION

SANJEEV
Acting Librarian
Central University of South Bihar

Ess Ess Publications
New Delhi

BASICS OF DIGITIZATION

ISBN : 978-81-934311-0-8

First Published 2017

Published by:
Ess Ess Publications
4831/24, Ansari Road,
Darya Ganj,
New Delhi-110 002.
INDIA
Phones: 23260807, 41563444
Fax: 41563334
E-mail: info@essessreference.com
www.essessreference.com

Cover Design by *Patch Creative Unit*

Printed and bound in India at Salasar Imaging Systems.

Dedicated to
MY PARENTS
&
FAMILY

Contents

1

Digitization

Technical Standards and Guidelines during digitization work are the essential issues of this process. It must be taken care during the planning stages. We should also discuss various techniques for creating digital files which are based on various guidelines. There may be valid institutional reasons for following or discarding different aspects especially in relation to the handling of original materials that may make certain processes unsuitable for that class of material. The fundamental issues associated with the digitization process are as follows:

KNOWLEDGE OF ORIGINAL DOCUMENTS

Having a good knowledge of the contents of the collections that are intended to be digitized will make it much easier to decide on processes and techniques for converting the originals to digital form. According to Dilip K. Swain and K. C. Panda in "An overview of Digitization of information resources" digitization is the quite simply the creation of a computerized representation of a printed analog. There are many methods of digitizing and varied media to be digitized. However, the main focus rests primarily on texts and images, as they are the main objects in the digitization process. The physical processes required to create a digitized version of an original item depend on many factors, including:

- The format of the original - is it printed text, photographic material, video, audio etc.?
- The condition of the original - will it stands up to automated procedures (if used), will conservation be required before scanning?
- The size of the original
- The color content of the original and whether those color is important.

For paper and photographic originals, issues to consider include the following:

Photographic media (transparencies, prints, and negatives)

- What size are the originals are they all the same size? It makes for a smoother workflow if items of a similar size are grouped together.
- What proportion of the items has color content? Is it important to capture the color?
- What condition are they in, for example, are they dirty from heavy use? If they are dirty a better scan will be achieved if the items can be cleaned first.
- What format are they in? Slides in sleeves or strips will take longer to prepare for scanning and may cost more if a bureau is scanning them. Glass negatives are prone to breakage and require careful handling.
- Are the photographs flat or have they bowed? Bowed originals cause difficulties with focus and may need weighting down.
- What is the quality of the original? A bad original (i.e. out of focus) will not be improved by scanning.

Paper media

- What size are the pages, are all items the same size?
- What general condition is the material in? Pristine pages will produce a better result and the scanning process may be able to be automated. Any damage in an original may be exacerbated by the scanning procedure.
- Can books that are bound be stripped to loose pages for scanning? Scanning from bound volumes is more complex and therefore expensive than from loose pages.
- Is there any artwork? - Is it black and white or color photographs or line art? Color scanning is generally more complex and resource intensive.
- Is the text size particularly small or large? Very small text may need a higher resolution to extract the information.
- Objects require a different approach. Artifacts, art works and sculptures cannot generally be successfully scanned using the techniques available for 'flat' media such as photographs. It will therefore be necessary to use photography, either traditional or digital, to get an image of the original.

DIGITIZATION: A TECHNICAL OVERVIEW

Digital preservation issues must be observed when producing digital content. A good baseline for creating a digital file that will be long-lasting and would be scan once for all purposes; this means that all the complex and expensive preparation work will only need to be done once. The digitization project should consider the value in creating a fully documented high-quality 'digital master file' from which all other versions (e.g. compressed versions for accessing via the Web) can be derived. This 'digital master file' should be created at the highest suitable resolution and bit depth that is both affordable and practical. This master file then becomes the source for every other version of that item that the project will require, such as Web surrogates, versions for high quality printing and so on. The 'digital master file' will become an archive version of the data - it remains as pure a representation of the original as possible. Ideally more than one copy should be stored on more than one media type and in more than one geographical location, thus providing a degree of protection against data corruption, media failure and physical damage to equipment. 'Surrogate' or 'access' versions of the digitized item can be created from the digital master file using image manipulation software such as Adobe Photoshop or Paintshop Pro. Commenting on the need of digital preservation John Ewing comments that reliance on past literature is common to all disciplines, but time scales differ. In some areas of science, literature more than a few years old has value mainly for historical reference.

BASIC STEPS OF DIGITIZATION

1. Identifying the documents to be digitized.
2. Selection of scanner from those available in the market as per needs.
3. Scanning of the document.
4. Selection of the format in which the scanned image is to be stored.
5. Selection of OCR and OWR devices to make the image browse able and scan able.
6. Organization of the digital content through any digital content management software.

FRAMEWORKS OF DIGITIZATION

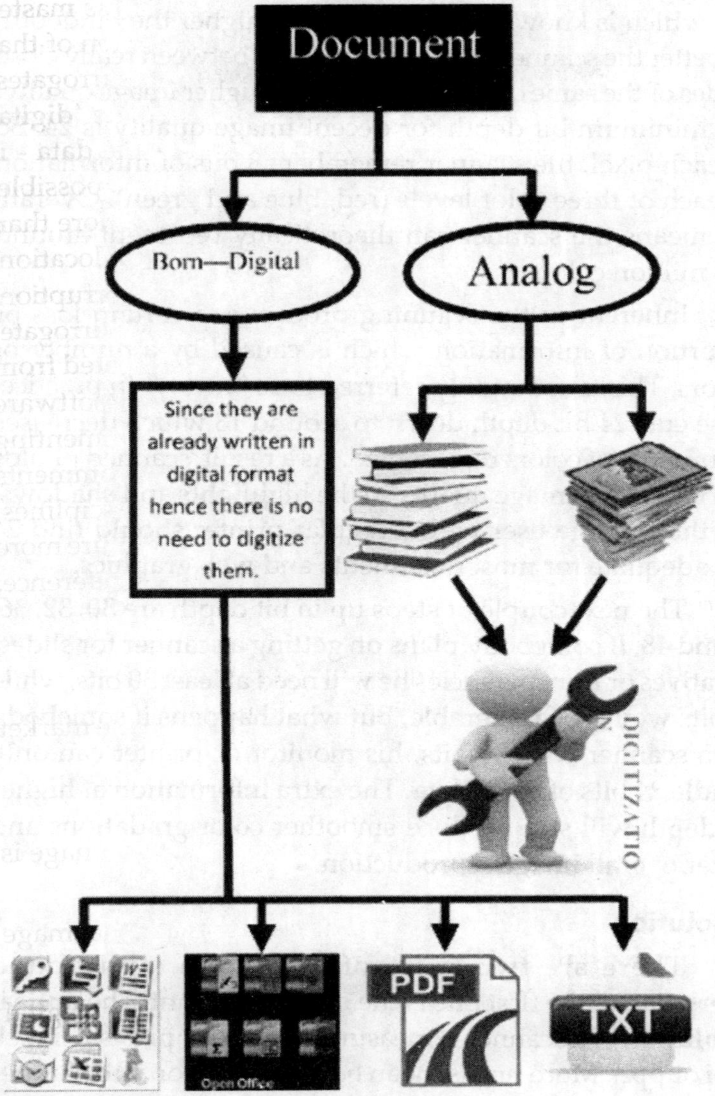

KEY FACETS OF DIGITIZATION

Bit Depth

It is essential to understand the term bit depth for knowing the complete process of scanning. For each pixel in an image, the scanner can remember a certain number of bits, which is known as bit depth. The higher the bit depth, the better the scanner is at distinguishing between really close shades of the same color. This results in higher image quality. The minimum bit depth for decent image quality is 24. So for each pixel, the scanner remembers 8 bits of information for each of three color levels (red, blue and green). Overall, this means the scanner can theoretically represent around 16.8 million colors.

Inherent in the scanning process is a certain loss or distortion of information which is caused by a number of factors. This is commonly referred to as "noise." In practice, noise cuts 24 bit depth down to around 18 which decreases the number of colors represented. As a result, scanned photos will lose some image quality in the highlights and shadows. But the average user with a regular printer should find 24 bits adequate for most documents and web graphics.

The next couple of steps up in bit depth are 30, 32, 36, 42 and 48. If somebody plans on getting a scanner for slides, negatives or transparencies he will need at least 30 bits, while 36 bits would be preferable. But what happens if somebody get a scanner with 30 bits, his monitor or printer can only handle 24 bits of color data. The extra information at higher bit depth will still produce smoother color gradations and better overall image reproduction.

Resolution

There are two types of resolution, optical and interpolated; the first one is the most important. The **optical resolution** of a scanner is measured in dots or pixels per inch (dpi or ppi). More pixels mean better resolution and sharper image quality. The number of pixels a scanner can generate is based on how many charged-couple devices (CCDs) are arranged horizontally and vertically in the scan head.

Remember one CCD produces one pixel. Resolution is quoted both horizontally and vertically (eg. 600x300). When comparing resolutions always use the smaller number. If you need to pick up fine details, small fonts or complex lines or edges more optical resolution you will require. Optical resolution is a more reliable indicator of the image quality.

For developing high quality image, the **interpolated resolution** of a scanner is always maintained higher than its optical resolution. For providing higher interpolated resolution, the scanner takes the information from two true pixels and by using mathematical algorithms it fills a third pixel between both of them. As more pixels are being mathematically generated and accommodated, the interpolated resolution becomes higher. Higher interpolated resolution will be sufficient if you just need to enlarge images.

An optical resolution of 300 dpi should be enough for the average user. It will produce an image that will look good on the web or printed out on an inkjet or laser printer. Graphic artists who want to scan line art or images with lots of detail will want to go up to 600 dpi. The people who are looking for a scanner to scan slides, negatives or transparencies need 1200 dpi resolution. Such a high resolution is needed to compensate for the small size of the original.

Even if the printer has lower resolution than by that particular scanner, scanning at higher resolutions will produce better image quality in the finished document. You will have to scan at higher resolution than what you want to print at because the image quality degrades when you process the image with editing software like PhotoShop. A scanner with a higher resolution will also produce better images even at resolutions below the maximum. For example, a 150 dpi scan from a 600 dpi scanner looks better than the same scan from a 300 dpi scanner.

Resolution Vs. Bit-depth

Resolution is usually expressed in dots per inch (DPI) and relates to the density of information that is captured by the scanning equipment. Broadly speaking, the higher the DPI the more detail is being captured. The amount of resolution required to get a useful image of an item is determined by the size of the original, the amount of detail in the original and the eventual use for the data. For example, a 35mm transparency will require a higher DPI than a 5x4 print because it is smaller and more detailed. An A4 sized modern printed document that is intended to be processed into a searchable text will need less resolution than a similar sized photographic original. There are also upward limits on resolution - file size is one (increasing resolution will increase the file size) and another is preventing the capture of extraneous information. For example, postcards are often printed on poor quality paper and if they are scanned at too high a resolution the texture of the paper will be captured and can obscure the content. There is also a point where putting more resolution into the capture process will no longer add value to the information content of the digital output. Suitable resolutions for digital master files for various media types are discussed in the HEDS Matrix and the JIDI Feasibility Study contains a useful table of baseline standards of minimum values of resolutions according to original material type. Bit-depth relates to the level of color that will be captured.

> A 'bit' is the binary digit that represents the total value of the pixel. As an overview, a 1-bit image is black and white (the pixel has 1 bit and is therefore black or white with no shades in between), an 8-bit image has 256 shades of either grey or color (28 = 256 shades), and a 24-bit image has millions of shades of color (224 = 16,777,216 shades).

A detailed discussion of resolution, binary and bit depth can be found on TASI's Web pages and a good basic guide to color capture can also be found on the EPIcentre Web pages.

In the process of creation of digital library we, information officers use to procure information in computer readable format, we organize it and maintain it for its best usage. For presenting an ideal example of digital library, it is essential to think about on our present text based collection and this is the real challenge for any practicing information officer. When we think about it, we need to convert all of this in the computer readable format while using latest tools and techniques of digitisation.

Dynamic Range or Optical Density

Those who need a good graphics scanner or want really high image quality, need to consider dynamic range, also called optical density (OD). It is a measure of how well the scanner can capture the tonal range of an image, the gradations from bright highlights all the way to dark shadows. Dynamic range is measured on a logarithmic scale (like the Richter scale) from 0-4 with zero as pure white and four as pure black. Dynamic range is the difference between the darkest and brightest optical densities a scanner can capture. The bigger the difference the larger the dynamic range.

Most flatbed scanners have an OD around 2.8-3.0 which is fine for the tonal range of photographs. To scan slides, negatives and transparencies which have broader tonal ranges, a higher OD will be required. For slides and transparencies OD must be around 3.2, a bit higher at 3.4 will be required for negatives. When comparing scanners with the same bit depth, choosing one with a higher dynamic range will give you better image reproduction.

Speed

Scanners for personal use won't be too concerned with

the speed. The speed depends on the scanning resolution, the higher the resolution lesser the speed. An efficient time for a 600 dpi colour scan is about 100 seconds but only 30 seconds for a monochrome 300 dpi scan.

Softwares

The software bundle probably contains

- Driver program,
- Color calibration software,
- Image-editing software and
- Optical recognition software (OCR).

For Windows operating system, the driver program of any scanner is usually TWAIN compatible. A TWAIN driver makes a scanner compatible with TWAIN-supported software. Since TWAIN has been emerged as an industry standard, most bundled software normally operate in the form of a TWAIN compatible solution. Color calibration software is used for maintaining the original colors of the image throughout its process of digitization. It enables us to have similar quality print out what we observes on the monitor of the system. Out of these varieties of software, Optical Recognition Software is most important for any information officer.

Optical Recognition Software (OCR)

"When a page of text is scanned into a PC, it is stored as an electronic file made up of tiny dots, or pixels; it is not seen by the computer as text, but rather, as a 'picture of text'. Word processors are not capable of editing bitmap images. In order to turn the group of pixels into editable words, the image must go through a complex process known as *Optical Character Recognition (OCR)*." (PC TechGuide, 2001). Optical recognition programs examine the scanned image and convert it into a format that can be read by a word processor, spreadsheet or database.

OCR research began in the late 1950s. According to PC TechGuide, "one of the earliest OCR techniques was something called matrix, or *pattern matching*. Most text is either in Times, Courier, or Helvetica typefaces in point sizes between 10 and 14. OCR programs, which use the pattern matching method, have bitmaps stored for every character of each of the different font and type sizes. By comparing a database of stored bitmaps distributed to the bitmaps of the scanned letters the program attempts to recognize the letters. This early system was only really successful using non-proportional fonts like Courier where letters are spaced regularly and are easier to identify. Complex multi-font documents were well beyond its scope and an obvious limitation to this method is that it is only useful for the fonts and sizes stored. *Feature extraction* was the next step in OCR's development. This attempted to recognise characters by identifying their universal features, the goal being to make OCR typeface-independent. If all characters could be identified using rules defining the way that loops and lines join each other, then individual letters could be identified regardless of their typeface. For example, the letter "a" is made from a circle, a line on the right side and an arc over the middle. The arc over the middle is optional. So, if a scanned letter had these "features" it would be correctly identified as the letter "a" by the OCR program. In terms of research progress, feature extraction was a step forward from matrix matching, but actual results were badly affected by poor-quality print. Extra marks on the page, or stains in the paper, had a dramatic effect on accuracy. The elimination of such "noise" became a whole research area in itself, attempting to determine which bits of print were not part of individual letters. Once noise can be identified, the reliable character fragments can then be reconstructed into the most likely letter shapes. No OCR software ever recognizes 100% of the scanned letters. Some OCR programs use the matrix/

pattern matching and/or feature extraction methods to recognize as many characters as possible and complement this by using spell checking on the hitherto unrecognized letters. For example, if the OCR program was unable to recognize the letter 'e' in the word 'their', by spell checking 'their' the program could determine the missing letter is an 'e'." (PC TechGuide, 2001).

Prominent features are:

- Text editing
- Word or phrase searching
- Compact storing
- Machine translation
- Text to speech conversion

Some of the OCR software are:

- Abby finereader
- Any Doc Software
- Brainware
- Open OCR
- OCRed
- Simple OCR
- Readinis
- Tesseract

ICR (Intelligent Character Reader) is an advanced OCR where handwriting recognition system is employed to improve accuracy and handwriting recognition levels of a computer. ICR has further matured to IWR (Intelligent Word Reader) that can recognize an extract printed handwritten information as well as cursive handwriting. Some of the software are Typereader, Abbi Finereader, A2ia document reader.

PC TechGuide further add that "recent OCR technology is far more sophisticated than the early techniques. Instead of just trying to identify individual characters, modern techniques are able to identify whole words. This technology, developed by *Caere,* is called *Predictive Optical Word Recognition (POWR).* Using higher levels of contextual analysis, POWR is able to virtually eliminate the problems caused by noise. It enables the computer to sift through the thousands or millions of different ways that dots in a word can be assembled into characters. Each possible interpretation is then assigned a probability, and the highest one is selected. POWR uses sophisticated mathematical algorithms which allow the computer to hone in on the best interpretation without examining each possible version individually. When probabilities are assigned to individual words, all kinds of contextual information and evidence is taken into account. The technology makes use of neutral networks and *predictive modelling techniques* taken from research in Artificial Intelligence (AI). These involve extensive use of *'experts'* - algorithms set up to be specialists in various areas of character recognition. One expert might know a great deal about font styles, another about dictionary information, another about the degradation caused by faxes. By combining the use of expert systems with modelling techniques taken from Cognitive Science, a mathematical, probabilistic infrastructure can be created that dynamically 'investigates' all the different possibilities of characters that make up a word in question by querying a variety of experts, and generating an initial set of general hypotheses. The evidence for and against each hypothesis is weighed and a probability assigned to each hypothesis. The investigation continues until a clear and compelling answer emerges. At each stage in the investigation, a new set of experts is selected based on the relevance of their areas of expertise to the particular situation." (PC TechGuide, 2001).

The net result is that POWR is able to identify words

in a way, which more closely resembles human visual recognition. In practice, the technique significantly improves the accuracy of word recognition across all document types. All the possible interpretations of a word are assessed by combining all sources of evidence, from low-level pixel-based information to high-level contextual clues. The most probable interpretation is then selected.

Although OCR systems have been around for a long time, their benefits are only just being appreciated. The first offerings were extremely costly, in terms of software and hardware, and they were inaccurate and difficult to use. Consequently many of the early adopters became frustrated with the technology. Over the past few years, however, OCR has been completely transformed. Modern OCR software is highly accurate, easy to use and affordable and for the first time OCR looks set to be adopted in all kinds of work environments on a mass scale.

Unless there is a specific need to preserve colour information from the original document, its best to scan documents for OCR in greyscale. This uses a third of the space of an RGB colour scan. Line-art mode makes for even smaller file sizes - but this often loses detail, reducing the accuracy of subsequent OCR processing.

Interface

Connecting a scanner to the computer can be done in a number of ways. Plugging a scanner into the parallel port and configuring it is fairly easy. Most of them come with pass-through connectors to attach the printer to the scanner, one should not try to use both at once. Parallel ports tend to be the slowest way to connect, but the latest models can be almost as fast as the other two options, USB and SCSI.

The Universal Serial Bus (USB) has become popular for offering straight-forward installation, flexible configuration and faster data transfer support.

Small Computer System Interface (SCSI) commonly known as scuzzy is a friendly solution and commonly used to connect high-end scanners. As it is connected through a port, this type of connection supports fast speed but normally it requires more work relating to configuration and installation.

Macintosh systems support SCSI connection. If somebody wants to get a SCSI scanner then he may have to open up the computer to install a SCSI controller card. Most SCSI scanners come with controller cards and SCSI cables. Even if he already has a SCSI card for another device, it may not be compatible with the scanner or the provided cables.

Scanning Process

According to PC TechGuide, all scanners work on the same principle of reflectance or transmission. The image is placed before the carriage, consisting of a light source and sensor; in the case of a digital camera, the light source could be the sun or artificial lights. When desktop scanners were first introduced, many manufacturers used fluorescent bulbs as light sources. While good enough for many purposes, fluorescent bulbs have two distinct weaknesses, they rarely emit consistent white light for long, and while lightening they emit heat which can distort the other optical components. For these reasons, most manufacturers have moved to 'cold-cathode' bulbs. These differ from standard fluorescent bulbs in that they have no filament. They therefore operate at much lower temperatures and, as a consequence, are more reliable. Standard fluorescent bulbs are now found primarily on low-cost units and older models.

By late 2000, Xenon bulbs had emerged as an alternative light source. Xenon produces a very stable, full-spectrum light source that's both long lasting and quick to initiate. However, xenon light sources do consume power at a higher rate than cold cathode tubes. To direct light from the bulb to the sensors that read light values, CCD scanners use prisms, lenses, and other optical components. Like eyeglasses and magnifying glasses, these items can vary quite a bit in quality. A high-quality scanner will use high-quality glass optics that are colour-corrected and coated for minimum diffusion. Lower-end models will typically skimp in this area, using plastic components to reduce costs.

The amount of light reflected by or transmitted through the image and picked up by the sensor, is then converted to a voltage proportional to the light intensity- the brighter the part of the image, the more light is reflected or transmitted, resulting in a higher voltage. This analogue-to-digital conversion (ADC) is a sensitive process, and one that is susceptible to electrical interference and noise in the system. In order to protect against image degradation, the best scanners on the market today use an electrically isolated analogue-to-digital converter that processes data away from the main circuitry of the scanner. However, this introduces additional costs to the manufacturing process, so many low-end models include integrated analogue-to-digital converters that are built into the scanner's primary circuit board.

The sensor component itself is implemented using one of three different types of technology:

- PMT, a technology inherited from the drum scanners of yesteryear
- CCD, the type of sensor used in desktop scanners
- CIS, a newer technology which integrates scanning functions into fewer components, allowing scanners to be more compact in size.

PMT

PMT (photomultiplier tube) is the sensor technology used by the high-end drum scanners used by colour prepress companies. Expensive and difficult to operate, these were the devices used to load images into a computer before the advent of desktop scanning.

Technicians would carefully mount originals onto a cylindrical drum which would then be spun at high speed. The machine would *PMT (photomultiplier tube)* is the sensor technology used by the high-end drum scanners used by colour prepress companies. Expensive and difficult to operate, these were the devices used to load images into a computer before the advent of desktop scanning.

Technicians would carefully mount originals onto a cylindrical drum which would then be spun at high speed. The machine would then be moved - via a mechanically accurate threaded shaft - initially to align its optical sensor with the original and then slowly across its entire span as the item was scanned. Variation to output size can be assisted with variable sideways carriage movement, different lenses for various reproduction ranges and different drum circumferences.

PMT scanners have two light sources, one for reflective original and one for transparent originals. The light detected by the sensor is split into three beams which are passed through red, green and blue filters and thence into the photomultiplier tubes - where the light energy is converted into an electrical signal. PMTs have a much higher sensitivity to light and lower noise levels than CCD scanners. Consequently, drum scanners are capable of excellent tonal resolution, being less susceptible to errors due to refraction or focus than their flatbed counterparts. However, drum scanners are slow compared to CCD scanners and are expensive. These days they're are generally used only for specialized high-end applications.

CCD

CCD (charge-coupled device) technology is responsible for having made scanning a desktop application and has been in use for a number of years in devices such as fax machines and digital cameras. A charge-coupled device is a solid state electronic device that converts light into an electric charge. A desktop scanner sensor typically has thousands of CCD elements arranged in a long thin line. The scanner shines light through red, green and blue filters and the reflected light is directed into the CCD array via a system of mirrors and lenses. The CCD acts as a photometer, converting the measured reflectance into an analogue voltage, which can then be sampled and changed to discrete digital values by an analogue-to-digital converter (ADC).

CIS

CIS (contact image sensor) is a relatively new sensor technology which began to appear at the budget end of the flatbed scanner market in the late 1990s. CIS scanners employ dense banks of red, green and blue LEDs to produce white light and replace the mirrors and lenses of a CCD scanner with a single row of sensors placed extremely close to the source image. The result is a scanner that is thinner and lighter, more energy efficient and cheaper to manufacture than a traditional CCD-based device - but that is not, as yet, capable producing as good results.

The technology employed by its sensor mechanism is not, however, the only factor that governs a scanner level of performance. The following are equally important aspects of a given unit's specification:

- resolution
- bit depth
- dynamic range

Scan resolution

Resolution relates to the fineness of detail that a scanner can achieve, and is usually measures in *dots per inch(dpi)*. The more dots per inch a scanner can resolve, the more detail the resulting image will have. The typical resolution of an inexpensive desktop scanner in the late 1990s was 300 x 300.

A typical flatbed scanner has a CCD element for each pixel, so for a desktop scanner claiming a horizontal optical resolution of 600 dpi(dots per inch) - alternatively referred to as 600 *ppi(pixels per inch)* - and a maximum document width of 8.5inch there will be an array of 5,100 CCD elements in what is known as the scan head.

The scan head is mounted on a transport which is moved across the target object. Although the process may appear to be a continuous movement, the head moves a fraction of an inch at a time, taking a reading between each movement. In the case of a flatbed scanner, the head is driven by a stepper motor, a device which turns a predefined amount and no more, each time an electrical pulse is fed.

The number of physical elements in a CCD array determines the x-direction sampling rate, and the number of stops per inch determines the y-direction sampling rate. Although these are conveniently referred to as a scanner's 'resolution', the term is not strictly accurate. The resolution is the scanner's ability to determine detail in an object and is defined by the quality of electronics, optics, filters and motor control, as well as the sampling rate.

The actual scan head, though capable of reading a raster line 8.5in wide, will be much smaller than that, typically around 4in wide. The reflected light is presented to the scan head through a lens, and the quality of the optics can have a greater effect on the resolution of the scan than the sampling rate. High resolution optics in a 400dpi scanner is likely to produce better results than a 600dpi device with poor optics.

By late 1998 the physical limit as to how many CCD elements could be placed side by side in one inch stood at 600. It is, however, possible for the apparent resolution to be increased using a technique known as interpolation, which under software or hardware control guesses intermediate values and inserts them between the real ones. Some scanners do this much more effectively than others.

The determination of the appropriate resolution at which to scan an image is important both in terms of achieving the desired quality and in terms of the efficiency of the scanning process itself. Since modern advertising has conditioned us to think that more is always better, it is not difficult to understand why many users have a tendency to scan at too high a resolution. The key point is that scan resolution should always be determined by the capability of the output device. If the chosen scan resolution does not properly match the given output device, there will be adverse consequences. If it is lower than the output resolution, the display or printing process will interpolate the extra pixels that are needed and the final result will lose detail and sharpness. If, on the other hand, the chosen scan resolution is higher than the output resolution, the display or printing process will discard the extra pixels. The result will look fine, but the same quality result could have been achieved with lower resolution and a smaller image file.

The following discusses rules for determining an appropriate scan resolution for each of:

- a glossy magazine
- an inkjet printer, and
- a computer monitor

Printed images use a technique called *halftoning* to reproduce different levels of colour. In magazines an ordered halftone is used, where regular dots of differing sizes produce the varying levels of colour. The typesetters used in offset lithography - the technology used for printing glossy magazines - are capable of printing at 133 lines per inch. This technology is not quite the same as laser or inkjet printer technology and the general rule here is for layout artists to scan at 1.5 times the printing resolution - an equivalent of

200dpi.

Most inkjet printers use *dithering*, where the dots are scattered across the area of each pixel. This produces better looking results at lower resolutions. The use of halftoning means that the number of pixels per inch the printer can reproduce is lower than its stated "dpi" resolution. When scanning for output on a printer, the scan resolution should match the intended output resolution as closely as possible, taking into account the relative sizes of the original and the reproduction. If these are to be the same, no adjustments are necessary. If, however, the scanned image is to be printed at a different size - either larger or smaller than the original - the scan resolution needs to be adjusted accordingly.

This is best illustrated by an example. Suppose the intention is to print the scan of a 1x1.5in stamp at a size of 2x3in on an inkjet printer that has a print resolution of 600dpi. If the stamp were to be scanned at a 600dpi resolution, the scanned image would have 600 pixels vertically (1in times 600dpi) and 900 pixels horizontally (1.5in times 600dpi). Enlarging the image to the intended print size of 2x3in reduces the effective resolution to 300dpi - the 900 horizontal pixels will be spread out over 3in (900 divided by 3 equals 300), and the same is true in the vertical dimension. This is only half of the printer's resolution and the output quality will be less than optimal. For the best quality final printed output - which actually uses the 600dpi resolution the inkjet is capable of - the image should be scanned at 1200dpi.

A similar adjustment needs to be made if the output size is smaller than the original. Suppose the intention is to scan a 4x5in cover that is to be displayed on a Web page at half size, 2x2.5in. Computer monitors typically have a resolution of 72 or 90dpi. Scanning the cover at 72dpi would produce an image with 288x360 pixels. Reducing this to half the size would still give an image with a vertical resolution of 144dpi, twice that necessary. In this example, therefore, the original image could be scanned at 36dpi with no loss of quality in the resultant displayed image.

The rules used in these examples can be summarised by the following formula:

SR = (DR x DW) / OW, where

SR = ideal scanning resolution, in dpi

DR = resolution of final display device, in dpi

DW = width at which the image will be printed or displayed, in inches

OW = width of the original being scanned, in inches.

Interpolation

Scanners typically offer resolutions of 2,400dpi, 4,800dpi and 9,600dpi. It is important to realise that scanners simply are not capable of picking up this level of detail. The actual optical resolution of the CCDs in most modern scanners is 600 x 1,200dpi at best and all higher figures are based on interpolation. Note that the specification of a *non-uniform resolution*, for example, 600 x 1200dpi - necessarily implies hardware interpolation, since the acquisition of data at 600dpi in one axis and 1200dpi in the other clearly cannot result in a 'square' of data. At 600 x 600dpi such a scanner will interpolate the 1200dpi dimension down to 600dpi (usually done by merely running the stepper motor that moves the light bar at twice its minimum rate), or at 1200 x 1200dpi they interpolate up the x dimension. Basically, an integrated circuit chip in the scanner generates new data by taking the dots the scanner actually sees, and calculating where the dots in between would most likely fall, using an algorithm to realise the colour of the new dots by averaging the colour of adjacent dots.

Software interpolation can increase the resolution even more than hardware interpolation. It is performed by the PC's processor under the control of the scanner's TWAIN driver software. Interpolated images will always seem too smooth and slightly out of focus. This doesn't matter so much with line-art where interpolation has the effect of smoothing out jagged edges. But for continuous-tone images like photographs, it is often better to stick with a scanner's actual optical resolution.

Colour scanners

Colour scanners have three light sources, one for each of red, green and blue primary. Some scanning heads contain a single fluorescent tube with three filtered CCDs, while others have three coloured tubes and a single CCD. The former produce the entire colour image in a single pass, the target being illuminated by the three rapidly changing lights, while the latter have to go back-and-forth three times.

Single-pass scanners have problems with the stability of light levels when they're being turned on and off rapidly. Older three-pass scanners used to suffer from registration problems along with being slow. More modern three-pass units are much improved and able to match some single-passers for speed. However, by the late 1990s most colour scanners were single-pass devices. These scanners use one of two methods for reading light values: *beam splitter* or *coated CCDs*. When a beam splitter is used, light passes through a prism and separates into the three primary scanning colours, which are each read by a different CCD. This is generally considered the best way to process reflected light, but to bring down costs many manufacturers use three CCDs, each of which is coated with a film so that it reads only one of the primary scanning colours from an unsplit beam. While technically not as accurate, this second method usually produces results that are difficult to distinguish from those of a scanner with a beam splitter.

Bit-depth Vs. Colored scanning

When a scanner converts something into digital form, it looks at the image pixel by pixel and records what it sees. That part of the process is simple enough, but different scanners record different amounts of information about each pixel. How much information a given scanner records is measured by its bit-depth.

The simplest kind of scanner only records black and white, and is sometimes known as a 1-bit scanner because each bit can only express two values, on and off. In order to see the many tones in between black and white, a scanner needs to be at least 4-bit (for up to 16 tones) or 8-bit (for up to 256 tones). The higher the scanner's bit-depth, the more accurately it can describe what it sees when it looks at a given pixel. This, in turn, makes for a higher quality scan. Most modern colour scanners are at least 24-bit, meaning that they collect 8 bits of information about each of the primary scanning colours: red, blue, and green. A 24-bit unit can theoretically capture over 16 million different colours, though in practice the number is usually quite smaller. This is near-photographic quality, and is therefore commonly referred to as "true colour" scanning.

Recently, an increasing number of manufacturers are offering 30-bit and 36-bit scanners capable, so they claim, of producing better quality colour images. Whilst the fact is that very few graphics software packages are capable of handling images with more than 24 bits, the additional bits are still worth having. When a software program opens a 30-bit or 36-bit image, it can use the extra data to correct for noise in the scanning process and other problems that hurt the quality of the scan. With more inherent information present in 30- and 36-bit scanned images, users can more precisely alter image detail and RGB luminance values via the scanner's driver software.

The alternative route to improved quality - simply by building better 24-bit scanners - that provide cleaner data, less affected by random noise in the lower-order bits - is actually much less economic. This approach would require highly precise optics for focusing reflected light to the CCDs (charge-coupled devices) that capture the data; minimal-distortion glass free from internal contaminants; CCDs that capture light and convert it to electrical signals with high accuracy; and a smoothly-moving scanning head with little vibration. Such a device would cost considerably more than one that used lower-cost and lower-quality components with slightly more expensive ADCs, capable of capturing 10-bits and 12-bits of data each - for the red, green and blue colour components respectively - rather than just 8.

Scan modes

PCs represent pictures in a variety of ways - the most common methods being are *line art, halftone, greyscale,* and *true colour*:

- *Line art* is the smallest of all the image formats. Since only black and white information is stored, the computer represents black with a 1 and white with a 0. It only takes 1-bit of data to store each dot of a black and white scanned image. Line art is most useful when scanning text or line drawing. Pictures do not scan well in line art mode.
- While computers can store and show greyscale images, most printers are unable to print different shades of grey. They use a trick called *halftoning*. Halftones use patterns of dots to fool the eye into believing it is seeing greyscale information
- *Greyscale* images are the simplest of images for the computer to store. Humans can perceive about 255 different shades of grey - represented in a PC by a single byte of data with the value 0 to 255. A greyscale

image can be thought of as equivalent to a black and white photograph

- *True colour* images are the largest and most complex images to store, PCs using 8-bits (1 byte) to represent each of the colour components (red, green, and blue) and therefore 24-bits in total to represent the entire colour spectrum.

TWAIN driver

TWAIN is known as an important standard in image processing and acquisition. It was jointly developed by *Hewlett-Packard, Kodak, Aldus, Logitech and Caere*. TWAIN standards allow software applications to work with image acquisition and processing devices without making itself aware about the peculiarities of the device itself. If the device and software application both are TWAIN compliant, the two should work together regardless the software was bundled with the image acquisition device.

It is possible to attach more than one TWAIN compliant image acquisition devices to a computer system at the same time. Each of these devices will have it's own separate TWAIN module. This makes it necessary for TWAIN compliant software applications to provide a means for the end user to select which TWAIN device to use during a session. In practice the "acquire" option in the File menu of an application such as PhotoShop would be selected. The user would be prompted to select a suitable TWAIN source which would launch the device's own driver, all without leaving the main application. After scanning, the driver automatically closes, leaving the scanned image open in the main application. No unnecessary quitting, launching, or saving of potentially large and possibly useless files.

Increasingly, manufacturers are shipping scanners with two TWAIN drivers. The first will be a basic, simplistic driver, aimed at the novice scanner. With this, scanning is basically a one-button affair. Click the preview button, and a small preview of the image appears on-screen, in a preview pane. From here, the scanning area may be adjusted along with the resolution and pixel depth. When completely happy with the preview results the Scan button is clicked to initiate the actual scan.

For more advanced there should be an Advanced Scanning Options button somewhere on the first driver. This will open the second driver, the one offering a higher degree of overall image adjustment such as brightness, contrast, colour and Gamma Correction. This allows adjustments to be made to specific ranges of tonal values, either as a whole, or to each primary colour in turn.

Color calibration

Any image scanned by desktop scanner can look different on screen than it does when printed, and both can vary quite a bit from the original. The solution to this problem is a colour calibration (or colour matching) system. Such software is really valuable only for scans of high-quality images (transparencies, professional-quality prints, etc.) that need to meet rigorous quality standards. For most people using a desktop scanner, accurate colour is not as important as fast, pleasing colour. This is just as well, as the complexities of colour and human perception have made calibration a daunting challenge and as a consequence, there are several different solutions already available, with more on the way. One of the most comprehensive systems is the *Kodak's Colour Management System (CMS)*, which uses its own colour definitions together with profiles for each different scanner, monitor, and printer in the system to translate and standardize colours. Elements of the Kodak system are bundled with Adobe PhotoShop and other software, and CMS is rapidly becoming the favorite of graphic artists and others who depend on closely matched colours. Other systems have been developed by individual scanner manufacturers and software publishers. These proprietary profile-based systems can also do the job, provided that they include profiles for all of the different devices that will be used for scanning, viewing, editing, and outputting the final image.

A final approach is known as output-based correction, and involves scanning and outputting a standard calibration target, and then making adjustments to colour profiles in order to standardize colours. This is a less sophisticated process, and is probably inappropriate for users who want to continually re-calibrate their systems for optimum results. For basic colour scanning, however, output-based correction is often sufficient.

Photo Retouching

While scanners provide an effective means of capturing colour images, that's often just the beginning. Once a photograph has been digitized, it's appearance can be dramatically altered by use of a bitmap editor or paint package.

In advertising and publishing, very few images are used 'raw-models' features are 'cleaned up', wrinkles ironed out, eyes sharpened and coloured, and untidy hair trimmed. There is also a trend towards producing attention-grabbing images by distorting and montaging elements of photographs.

Generally the photo-retoucher is trying to do one of two things - change some elements of a picture in a natural way that cannot be detected (like changing the colour of someone's eyes) or produce something unreal and impossible-looking. Either way, the hand of the retoucher must be invisible.

Most of this kind of work is produced using Adobe PhotoShop, but even the simplest paint packages allow these kinds of alterations. However, while a lot can be achieved with the cheaper packages such as PaintShop Pro and PC Paintbrush, packages like PhotoShop, Xres and Corel PhotoPaint make complicated effects much easier to achieve.

Maintenance Aspect

For cleaning the scanner's glass bed of any scanner use mild soap or an ordinary glass cleaner. Put it on a soft cloth, do not pour it on the glass. Whatever you do, do not get the 'inch' ruler scales wet enough to damage them. The bottom of the rulers is often used for the scanner's internal calibration area before beginning a scan. Don't do anything foolish or excessive in that area. Don't get the glue wet either. Don't pour the cleaning fluid directly on the glass bed due to this risk. Instead put it on the cloth and then wipe with the cloth. You don't notice this film on windows or mirrors, but the scanner's bright light causes the scans to show it. It can cause some odd 'oily' or speckled effects in your scans from such residue between the photo and the glass. Be careful to inspect the glass closely under the scanner's bright light to be certain all of the cleaner film is removed. Inspect the glass (down low from the side) in the bright light for streaks, to make sure you have removed all of it.

Whatever you do, do not scratch the glass. Paper towels are rough, and can make fine scratches on optical surfaces (for example, you would never consider using paper towels on a camera lens), and a soft cloth should be used instead. It would be wrong to recommend it, but I admit that I do use the better softer paper towels on the scanner bed. But I apply them 'easy' without much pressure. Whatever you use, crumple it up real good so that any grit hopefully can find a crevice to get into, away from the glass. Grit is a real issue, keep that in mind, and don't scrub hard.

To check your work, open or remove the scanner's lid, and scan a large area of 'nothing'. Don't put anything on the glass, simply scan nothing with the lid off or fully open. 100 dpi is more than enough. You will get an all-black image, there is nothing to reflect the light back to the scanner. View it both at Actual image size, and also view it reduced to fit on the screen. See any faint haze or cloudy areas?

Then you didn't do a good job cleaning the glass. White spots seen there may be dust on the glass, or may be noise. Dust is spots in repeatable locations, noise spots will vary from scan to scan.

Vernon Kinslow suggested as "An old clean diaper or an old clean T-shirt leaves very few lint specks. Also if you clean one side right to left and the other side up and down, if you leave a streak you can go straight to it and correct the problem." This is surely better than a paper towel, but any grit can still scratch.

Normally the scanner's top cover is removed very easily, for the purpose of cleaning the bottom side of the glass. Be certain to unplug the power cord first. There is high voltage on the lamp and line voltage too. Stick to the purpose of cleaning the glass and leave the rest alone.

PIM technology

In 1998, the Photographic Industry Association comprising most of the world's digital camera manufacturers came up with a set of standards called the *Design Rule for Camera File System (DCF)*. This defined colour parameters for digital camera images which took into account the limited colour range supported by the WWW and computer display monitors. This digital camera image 'target colour space' was, in fact, identical to the sRGB colour space originally developed by Microsoft Corporation and Hewlett Packard in the mid-1990s. The implications of this were that after being shot, an image's hues were compressed by a digital camera to make them fit within the DCF-defined colour spectrum.

The DCF colour standard worked well enough until early in the new millennium. However, by then the sRGB colour space was not as large, nor as rich in colour as the spectrum available on even the inexpensive photo-printers of the day. Users were thus being deprived of the opportunity to produce output with the nuances of colour their equipment was capable of.

In early 2001 Epson unveiled a solution to this problem, in the shape of its *Print Image Matching (PIM) technology*. PIM works within the structure of DCF, while allowing devices with extended colour capabilities to print the greater spectrum of colour captured by a digital camera. It does this by getting a digital camera to store the complete colour information for a captured image before it is converted to the DCF standard. When images are output to a printer the PIM printer driver software reads the associated PIM data, thereby allowing them to be reproduced with the extended range of colour. PIM doesn't interfere with a digital camera's operation in any way. Specifically, it has no impact on image processing and therefore shot-to-shot time. Indeed, users can turn PIM off if it is not required. In the event that images shot with PIM enabled are subsequently transferred to software applications or printers that don't support PIM, the PIM data is simply ignored.

PIM can be viewed as both an open and adaptable standard. Open in as much as the technology is available to any printer manufacturer who chooses to license it and adaptable since it can evolve as CCD sensors and printers improve, ensuring that the colour fidelity of printed images will continue to be preserved in the future. It also offers the prospect of digital camera manufacturers being able to add user selectable image enhancements for use at picture taking time, allowing photographers to preset the intensities of such controls as contrast, colour balance, highlight point, shadow point, brightness, saturation, and sharpness to suit their personal preferences.

X3 technology

In 2002 after five years of research and development, the prospect of digital cameras with affordable film-quality was given a massive boost when Foveon Corporation unveiled a digital camera imaging sensor which the company claimed was capable of obviating 35mm film. In conventional digital cameras systems colour filters are applied to a single layer of photo-detectors in a tilted mosaic pattern.

The filters let only one wavelength of light i.e. red, green or blue pass through to any given pixel, allowing it record only one colour. As a result, typical mosaic sensors capture 50% of the green and only 25% of each of the blue and red light. The approach has inherent drawbacks, no matter how many pixels a mosaic-based image sensor might contain. Since they only capture one third of the colour, mosaic-based image sensors must rely on complex processing to interpolate the two-thirds they miss. Not only does this slow down the speed of image rendering, interpolation also leads to colour artifacts and a loss of image detail. Some cameras even intentionally blur pictures to reduce colour artifacts.

Foveon's new CMOS image sensor uses the company's revolutionary *X3 technology* to capture up to three times more information per pixel than modern day digital cameras at similar mega pixel resolutions. The X3 image sensors accomplish this by using three layers of photo detectors embedded in silicon. The layers are positioned to take advantage of the fact that silicon absorbs different colours of light at different depths, so one layer records red, another layer records green and the remaining layer records blue. This means that for every pixel on a Foveon X3 image sensor, there's actually a stack of three photo detectors. The result is a sensor capable of capturing red, green, and blue in each pixel location in essence, the first full-colour digital camera image sensor.

Foveon's X3 technology not only leads to better pictures, but better cameras too. In fact, it opens the door to an entirely new breed of camera, one that can switch seamlessly between still photography and digital video, without sacrificing the quality of either. Because *Foveon* X3 image sensors capture full colour at every pixel location, those pixels can be grouped together to create larger, full-colour '*super pixels*'. This capability, called *Variable Pixel Sizing (VPS)*, marks another first in digital photography.

With VPS, the signals from groups of pixels can be combined so the camera reads them as one. For example, a 2300x1500 image sensor contains more than 3.4 million pixels. But if VPS is used to group those pixels into 4x4 blocks, the image sensor would appear to have 575x375 pixels, each of them 16 times larger than the originals. The size and configuration of a pixel group is variable - 2x2, 4x4, 3x5, etc. and is controlled through sophisticated circuitry integrated into Foveon X3 image sensors.

The grouping of smaller pixels into larger pixels increases the signal-to-noise ratio. This allows the camera to take full-colour pictures in low-light conditions with reduced noise. Using VPS to reduce the resolution also allows the sensor to run at higher frame rates, accelerating the rate at which pictures can be taken. These gains in speed and sensitivity offer other benefits such as an improved focusing system.

VPS also makes it possible to switch from high-quality still photography to outstanding digital video, enabling the development of the first cameras with true dual-mode functionality. Hitherto, cameras attempting to accommodate both still and video functions have had to sacrifice performance in one mode to do the other well. The unique design of Foveon X3 image sensors enables them to handle both functions without compromise.

REFERENCES

Owen, Mackenzie (2007), The Scientific article in the age of digitization, O.S. Springer. Smithsonisn Institute (2005), Digitization

National Library of Canada (1995), Digitization: selected background papers, National Library of Canada

Koelling, Marie Jill (2004), Digital imaging: a practical approach, Rowman Altamira.

Lee, Stuart D (2001), Digital imaging: a practical handbook, Neal-Schuman Publishers.

Anderson, Cokie (2006), Ethical decision for digital libraries, Chandos Publications

Polostron, Lucien (2009), The great digitization: and the quest to know everything, X. Inner Traditions

Edwing, John (2011), Twenty centuries of mathematics: digitizing and disseminating the past mathematical literature, http://eprints.rclis.org

Lahiri, A. (2001), Digitization – A new mandate. Information today and tomorrow, Vol. 20 (2), 2001, p.1-2

Gonalez, R.C. and Woods, R. E. (2002), Digital Image Processing, Prentice-Hill, 2002

Kuny T. and Cleveland G. (2011), The digital library: myths and challenges, IFLA Journal, Vol. 24 No 2, pp.107-13

Husler, R.P. (2011), Digital library: content preservation in digital world, DESIDOC Bulletin of information technology, vol. 16 no. 1, pp. 31-9.

Yerkley, A.N. and Joirgensin, C. (2009), A course in digital libraries, Vol.16 no.1, pp.31-9.

ARL (1996), Spec Kit 214: Digitizing technology for preservation. ARL, 1996.

Ewing, John (2010), E-prints in Library and Information Science, http://eprints.rclis.org/archive/00001381/01/Twenty_centuries.pdf

PC TechGuide (2001) Scanner. http://rays-place.net/Extras/PCTechGuide/ 18scanners.htm

2

Tools of Digitization

The term photography is derived from the greek word. Sir John Herschel was the first person who used the term "Photography". In the year 1839 the process of photography became publicly popular. Photography is a process which involves two distinct scientific processes. These scientific processes are related to the capturing and storing of images.

PINHOLE CAMERA

A pinhole camera, also known as camera obscura, or "dark chamber", is a simple optical imaging device in the shape of a closed box or chamber. In one of its sides is a small hole which, via the rectilinear propagation of light, creates an image of the outside space on the opposite side of the box.

In case of Pinhole camera, Images created via a small opening will be found in the natural environment and in everyday life. This type is very popular in various parts of the world since ancient period. Probably the earliest surviving description of this kind of observation dates from the 5th century BC, written by Chinese philosopher Mo Ti. In the Western hemisphere, Aristotle in 4 BC was asking, without receiving any satisfactory answer, why sunlight passing through quadrilaterals. In 10 AD the Arabian physicist and mathematician Ibn al-Haitham, known as Alhazen, studied the reverse image formed by a tiny hole and indicated the rectilinear propagation of light. There was another scholar during the Middle Ages who was familiar with the principle of the camera obscura, namely the English monk, philosopher and scientist Roger Bacon. It was not until the manuscript *Codex atlanticus* (c. 1485) that the first detailed description of the pinhole camera was set down by Italian artist and inventor

Leonardo da Vinci, who used it to study perspective.

***Source*: website instruction tables (2011)**

Pinhole camera is a smaller version of that room, and the **film** inside the camera replaces human memory. The film records the image through the pinhole. The pinhole forces every point emitting light in the scene to form a small point on the film, so the image is crisp. The reason a normal camera uses a lens rather than a pinhole is because the lens creates a much larger hole through which light can make it onto the film, due to which the film is exposed faster. The photographer exposes the film for a long time because the pinhole lets so little light through. In the pinhole camera the pinhole acts as the **lens**.

TWIN-LENS REFLEX (TLR) CAMERAS

Double-lens cameras seem first to have been developed around 1870, when it was realized that having a second lens alongside the taking lens meant that one could focus without having to keep swapping a ground glass screen for the plate afterwards, making the time delay in actually taking the shot rather less(1). This sort of approach was still used as late as the 1960s, as the monstrous Koni-Omegaflex testifies. A twin-lens reflex camera (TLR) is a type of camera with two objective lenses of the same focal length. One of the lenses is the photographic objective or "taking lens" (the lens that takes the picture), while the other is used for the viewfinder system, which is usually viewed from above at waist level. Besides fulfilling the basic objective, the viewfinder consists of a 45-degree mirror (that is why the word *reflex* is in the name), a matte focusing screen at the top of the camera, and a pop-up hood surrounding it.

***Source*: website of sheldonbrown (2011)**

Higher-end Twin Lens Reflex (TLR) Camera may have a pop-up magnifying glass to assist the user in focusing the camera. In addition, many have a "sports finder" consisting of a square hole punched in the back of the pop-up hood, and a knock-out in the front. A photographer can sight through these instead of using the matte screen. This is especially useful in tracking moving subjects since the image on the matte screen is reversed left-to-right.

Many TLRs used front and back cut-outs in the hinged top hood to provide a quick-action finder for sports and action photography. Late model Rollei Rolleiflex TLRs introduced the widely-copied additional feature of a second-mirror "sports finder". When the hinged front hood knock-out is moved to the sports finder position a secondary mirror swings down over the view screen to reflect the image to a secondary magnifier on the back of the hood, just below the direct view cutout. This permits precise focusing while using the sports finder feature. The magnified central image is reversed both top-to-bottom and left-to-right. Due to this feature, Rolleis has become the leading choice of press photographers during 1940s to 1960s.

The typical TLR is medium format, using 120 roll film with square 6×6 cm images. Presently, only the Chinese Seagull Camera is still in production, but in the past, many manufacturers made them. The Ciro-flex produced by Ciro Cameras Inc. rose dramatically in popularity due in large part to the inability to obtain the German Rollei TLRs during World War II. The Ciro-flex was widely accessible, inexpensive, and produced high quality images. Models with the Mamiya, Minolta and Yashica brands are common on the used-camera market, and many other companies made TLRs that are now classics. The Mamiya C series TLRs had interchangeable lenses, allowing focal lengths from 55mm (wide angle) to 250mm (telephoto) to be used. The bellows focusing of these models also allowed extreme close-ups to be taken, something difficult or impossible with most TLRs. The simple, sturdy construction of many TLRs means they have tended to endure the years well. Many low-end cameras used cheap shutters however, and the slow speeds on these often stick or are inaccurate.

There were smaller TLR models, using 127 roll film with square 4×4 cm images, most famous the "Baby" Rolleiflex and the Yashica 44. The TLR design was also popular in the 1950s for inexpensive fixed focus cameras such as the Kodak Duaflex and Argus 75. Though most used medium format film, a few 35mm TLRs were made, the Contaflex TLR being the most elaborate, with interchangeable lenses and removable backs.

The smallest general-use TLR camera is the Swiss-made Tessina, using perforated 35mm film forming images of 14×21 mm. It has been argued that the "business end" of the Olympus Gastro Camera is technically the smallest actual TLR device.

SINGLE-LENS REFLEX (SLR) CAMERA

Digital single-lens reflex (SLR) cameras are the standard tool for professional photographers. With the introduction of cameras such as the Nikon D40/D40x (current entry-level model is the Nikon D3000) and the Canon Digital Rebel XTi (current entry-level model is the Canon Rebel T3), the market for digital SLR cameras has expanded tremendously. A point-and-shoot compact digital camera can offer reasonably good image quality, but a digital SLR, which usually looks a lot like an old standard 35mm film camera and may use the same lenses, offers the various advantages including:

- Accurate, large, and bright optical viewfinder.
- Fast operation and fast controls.
- Excellent image quality in low light situations when it is necessary to use higher ISO speeds.
- Interchangeable lenses

The single lens reflex (SLR) cameras are serious camera, in these cameras same lens is used for viewing and for taking photographs. A mirror in the body directs the light from the lens up into a prism for viewing, and then flips up out of the way just before an exposure is made. Professional photographer's or standard photo journalist's Nikon from the 1960s or 1970s was an SLR camera with a roll of 35mm film behind the mirror. When the mirror came up the light passed through to the shutter, which opened to expose one frame of film for perhaps 1/60th of a second. A Canon Digital Rebel or Nikon D80 looks very similar and works in almost the same way. The only difference is that instead of a piece of film behind the shutter there is an electronic sensor.

The mirror and optical viewfinder are what enable a photographer to frame images more quickly and accurately than with a point-and-shoot camera. Regardless of what lens or filters photographer has attached to the camera he/she see what the sensor will see. The typical digital SLR camera viewfinder offers additional information underneath the image, including all the most important camera settings.

***Source*: website 3dmodelfree (2011)**

A digital SLR may offer the same number of megapixels, individual image elements, as a high-end point-and-shoot. Not all pixels are created equal, however. Resolution is important if you intend to make large prints but dynamic range, the ability to capture detail within bright highlights and dark shadows, is more critical in many situations. The sensors in digital SLRs are typically much larger than those found in point-and-shoot cameras. The main advantage of a larger sensor is better performance in dim light. If there are 8 megapixels spread out over a sensor that is 4 times larger than the sensor in a point-and-shoot camera that means more photons of light will fall on any given pixel. If during an exposure 50 photons would fall on the small sensor then 200 photons would fall on the big sensor. If there is a small change in the light from one part of the scene to another the sensor in the point and shoot camera is trying to notice a single extra photon; the electronics in the camera with the big sensor have four extra photons that are much easier to detect.

There are three kinds of digital SLR systems being made as of September 2005 :

- Big lenses, big sensor
- Big lenses, small sensor
- Small lenses, small sensor

BIG LENSES, BIG SENSOR

Canon and Kodak have taken the most obvious approach to the challenge of transitioning from film to digital: build a digital sensor exactly the same size as one frame of 35mm film. The result is a chunk of silicon 24x36mm in size, which is vast compared to the sensor in a point-and-shoot digicam. The benefit of this vast sensor is reduced noise, which looks like grain, in low light/high-ISO situations. The drawback of a vast sensor is that manufacturing a flawless piece of silicon this big is very expensive. Consumer-priced cameras in this category include: Canon EOS 5D, Canon EOS 5D Mark II, Nikon D700, Nikon D3 and Sony Alpha A900. If one has a strong back and an unlimited budget, the Canon EOS 1Ds Mark III is a great choice. It is probably the best digital camera made and produces image quality that rivals medium format film (e.g., 6x6cm Hasselblad). The only other full-frame digital SLRs made were the discontinued Kodak DCS Pro SLR/n and SLR/c bodies.

BIG LENSES, SMALL SENSOR

Most of the digital Single Lens Reflux cameras fall into this category. The front part of the body use to have same lens mount. The back part of the camera has a sensor which is moderately smaller than 24x36mm standard frame. Due to this new design, the camera looks like an old film camera but it multiplies the magnification with the help of new and modified lenses. One does not require capturing the complete information on the extreme left and right, similarly extreme top and bottom of the frame. For capturing in digital file, what we see optically is more essential and thus viewfinder is provided for making required adjustments. If the photographer belongs to the moving film photography, he may feel difficulty and do require to some fresh mental and psychological adjustments. A 50 mm normal lens on a big lens/small sensor camera use to behave like a 80 mm tele-photo lens in a film camera. A 20 mm ultra wide angle lens use to behave like a 30-32 mm little bit wider angle lens on a film camera. Normally most of the popular digital SLR cameras belong to this category.

SMALL LENSES, SMALL SENSOR

The biggest problem with the "big lens, small sensor" situation is that photographers are forced to cart around lenses that are much larger, heavier, and, theoretically, more expensive, than they need to be. This has led to the introduction of lenses that have the big lens mount for a 35mm film camera but optically cover only the small sensor of a mid-range digital SLR. These are sold as "digital-only lenses" or "digital camera lenses" but in fact they won't work on a full-frame digital SLR. (Greenspun, 1997)

CAMERA LENS

The camera lens is an invention that attempts to duplicate the operation of the human eye. Just like the eye, the lens sees an image, focuses it, and transmits its colors, sharpness, and brightness through the camera to the photographic film, which, like our memory, records the image for processing and future use. Lenses are made of optical glass or plastic. They focus light rays by refracting or bending them so that they meet or converge at a common point. A simple lens "sees" well through its center, but its vision around the edges tends to blur. Blurring, color changes, distortion of lines, and color halos around objects are caused by defects in the lens called aberrations. Some aberrations can be corrected in the simple lens by shaping one or both surfaces so they are aspheric; aspheric curves vary like the curves of a parabola, rather than staying constant like the curvature of a sphere. A camera lens reduces the effects of aberrations by replacing a simple lens with a group of lenses called lens elements, which are lenses of different shapes and distances of separation.

The lens becomes more complex as greater correction of vision is achieved. The lens will also be more complex depending on the size of the aperture, the opening that allows light to pass through and the range of angles it "sees". Lens design used to rely on the optician's art and considerable experimentation. Now-a-days computer programs can adjust the shaping and spacing of lens elements, determine their effects on each other, and evaluate costs of lens production.

Lens elements are usually described by their shape. The convex lens curves outward; a biconvex lens curves outward on both sides, and a plano-convex lens is flat on one side and outwardly curved on the other. There are also concave lenses, biconcave, and plano-concave lenses. The elements are not necessarily symmetrical and can curve more on one side than the other. Thickening the middle of the lens relative to its edges causes light rays to converge or focus. Lenses with thick edges and thin middles make light rays disperse. A complex camera lens contains a number of elements specially grouped. The combination of the composition, shape, and grouping of the elements maximizes the light-bending properties of the individual elements to produce the desired image. The lens is focused by moving it nearer or farther from the film or focal plane. The lens can be twisted, causing the lens elements to move in and out along a spiral screw thread machined into the casing of the lens. Twisting the lens also moves a scale on the casing that shows the distance of the best focus.

The stop or diaphragm is a specialized part of the lens. In simple cameras, the stop is a fixed stop or a ring of black sheet metal that is permanently set in front of the lens. Box cameras, studio cameras, and some cameras of European manufacture use a sliding stop, which is a strip of metal that slides across the front of the lens between grooves. It has two or more holes of different sizes that are the apertures. Lenses with a variable stop have a machined ring on the outside of the lens mount, printed with f-stop numbers. By turning this ring, the diaphragm can be opened or closed. This iris diaphragm works much like the iris of the eye in allowing adjustments for varied light conditions.

The lens in a compact camera is usually a general-purpose lens with a normal focal length that takes pictures of an image the way our eyes see it. Lenses designed for special purposes are used with more advanced cameras. Telephoto lenses work like binoculars or telescopes, and make a distant image appear closer. Wide-angle lenses make the image appear farther away; a panoramic lens is a special kind of wide-angle lens that is useful for taking pictures of broad expanses of scenery. Some disposable cameras are equipped with panoramic lenses. A fish-eye lens is also a special kind of wide-angle lens that deliberately distorts the image so the central part is enlarged and the outer image details are compressed. Fish-eye lenses cover very wide angles like horizon-to-horizon views. Another special purpose lens is the variable-focus lens, also called a "zoom" lens. It uses moveable lens elements to adjust the focal length to zoom closer to or farther away from the subject. These lenses are complex and may contain 12 to 20 lens elements; however, one variable-focus lens may replace several other lenses. Some compact cameras also have limited zoom, telephoto, or wide-angle features.

The lens of the camera evolved from optical lenses developed for other purposes, and matured with the camera and photographic film. In 1568, a Venetian nobleman, Daniel Barbaro, placed a lens over the hole in a camera box and studied sharpness of image and focus. His first lens was from an old man's convex spectacles. The astronomer Johann Kepler elaborated on Barbaro's experiments in 1611 by describing single and compound lenses, explaining image reversal, and enlarging images by grouping convex and concave lenses.

During 1800s, the first box cameras had a lens mounted in the opening in the box. The lens inverted the image on a light-sensitive plate at the back of the box. There was no shutter to open the lens; instead, a lens cap was removed for several seconds or longer to expose the plate. Improvements in the sensitivity of the plate necessitated ways of controlling the exposure. Masks with different sized openings were made for insertion near the lens. The iris diaphragm was also developed to control the aperture. Its metal leaves open and close together to form a circular opening that can be varied in diameter.

In 1841, Joseph Petzval of Vienna designed a portrait lens with a fast aperture. Previously, lenses made for daguerreotype cameras were best suited for landscape photography. Petzval's lens allowed portraits to be taken ten times faster, and the photograph was less likely to be blurred. In 1902, Paul Rudolph developed the Zeiss Tessar lens, considered the most popular ever created. In 1918, he produced the Plasmat lens, which may be the finest camera lens ever made. Rudolph was followed shortly by Max Berek, who designed sharp, fast lenses that were ideal for miniature cameras. Other essential developments in lens history include lens coating technology, use of rare-earth glass, and calculation methods made possible by the computer. Katharine B. Blodgett developed techniques for thin-coating lenses with soap film to remove reflection and improve light transmission in 1939. C. Hawley Cartwright continued Blodgett's work by using coatings of metallic fluorides, including evaporated magnesium and calcium that were four-one-millionths of an inch thick.

Design of a camera lens begins by identifying the user of the camera. Being a user based product, it is essential to identify the market or various types of user groups. With its identification, we can a camera designer may identify following issues:

- Specifications of the technology
- Design of external body
- Expected requirements of the output

Due to technological advancements, a number of technological solutions are available. It is the requirement of user, which gives us support/blueprint in customizing the new product for the market.

The lens designer selects the optical and mechanical materials, the optical design, the appropriate method for making the mechanical parts, and, for auto focus lenses, the type of inter-face between the lens and camera. There are conventions or patterns for the different categories of lenses, including macro, wide-angle, and telephoto lenses, so some design aspects are standardized.

The group of lenses is called lens elements, which are of different shapes and distances of separation, make up the camera lens. Lens design used to rely on the optician's art and considerable experimentation. Today, computer programs can adjust the shaping and spacing of lens elements, determine their effects on each other, and evaluate costs of lens production. In selecting materials, the engineer must consider a range of metals for the components and various types of glasses and plastics for the lenses etc. When the designer completes the design, its performance is tested by computer simulation. Computer programs that are specific to lens manufacturers tell the designer what kind of image or picture the lens will produce at the center of the image and at its edges for the range of lens operation. Assuming the lens passes the computer simulation test, the criteria for performance that were chosen initially are reviewed again to confirm that the lens meets the needs identified. A prototype is manufactured to test actual performance. The lens is tested under varying temperature and environmental conditions, at every aperture position, and at every focal length for zoom lenses. Target charts in a laboratory are photographed, as are field conditions of varying light and shadow. Some lenses are aged rapidly in laboratory tests to check their durability.

After completing this process, additional design work is needed if the lens focuses automatically, because the auto focus (AF) module must work with a range of camera bodies. The AF module requires both software and mechanical design. Extensive prototype testing is performed on these lenses because of their complex functions and because the software is fine-tuned to each lens. For developing the complete set of lenses, the specific raw material including the lenses themselves, the coating, the barrel, or housing for the camera lens, and lens mounts are essential.

MANUFACTURING PROCESS OF CAMERA LENSES

Optical glass is supplied normally provided by lens manufacturer in the form of a "pressed plate" or sliced glass plate from which the elements are cut. The glass elements are shaped to concave or convex forms by a curve generator machine that is a first-step grinder. To reach the specifications for its shape, a lens goes through a sequence of processes in which it is ground by polishing particles in water. The polishing particles become smaller in each step as the lens is refined. Curve generation and subsequent grinding vary in speed depending on the frailty, softness, and oxidation properties of the optical materials. After grinding and polishing, the elements are centered so that the outer edge of the lens is perfect in circumference relative to the centerline or optical axis of the lens. Lenses made of plastic or bonded glass and resin are also produced by the same processes. Bonded materials are used to make lenses with non-spherical surfaces, and these lenses are called "hybrid asphericss". The aspherical surfaces of these lenses are completed during centering. (Holmes, 1996)

After completing the process of developing specific lenses, lenses are coated for getting protected from oxidation, to prevent reflections, and to meet requirements for "designed spectrum transmission" or color balance and rendition. The lens surfaces are carefully cleaned before coating. Techniques for applying coatings and the coatings themselves are very important issues for developing quality product. Some types of coatings include metal oxides, light-alloy fluorides, and layers of quartz that are applied to lenses and mirrors by a vacuum process. Several layers of coating may be applied for the best color and light transmission, but excessive coating can reduce the light that passes through the lens and limit its usefulness. The barrel of the ready lens includes the chassis that supports the various lens elements and the cosmetic exterior. Metal mounts, grooves, and moving portions of the lens are critical to the performance of the lens, and are machined to very specific tolerances. Lens mounts may be made of brass, aluminum, or plastic. Most metal barrel components are die-cast and machined. Metal mounts last longer, maintain their dimensions, can be machined more precisely, and can be dismantled to replace elements, if necessary. Plastic mounts are less expensive and of lighter weight. If the barrel is made of engineering plastic, it is produced by a highly efficient and precise method of injection molding. The interior surfaces of the barrel are also coated to protect them and to prevent internal reflection and flare. (Holmes, 1996)

Other parts of the lens, such as the diaphragm and auto focus module, are produced as subassemblies. The iris diaphragm is constructed of curved leaves cut out of thin sheets of metal. The metal leaves are held in place by two plates. One plate is fixed, the other moves, and has slots for sliding pins. These slide the leaves back toward the barrel to open the diaphragm or into the center to close the opening as the f-stop ring is turned. The diaphragm assembly is fastened into place when the lens mount is attached to the end of the barrel. The auto focus is also added, the optical elements are positioned, and the lens is sealed. After final assembly, the lens is adjusted and inspected rigorously. It must meet the design standards for optical resolution, mechanical function, and auto focus response. Lenses may also be tested by subjecting them to shocks, dropping, and vibration.

For developing quality lenses some of the manufacturers use full automation including industrial robots to make their products, others use large assembly lines, and still others pride themselves on hand-crafting. Quality and precision are essential to lens production, however, regardless of manufacturing approach. Incoming materials and components are rigorously inspected for quality and compliance with engineering specifications. Automated processes are also inspected constantly and subjected to tolerance checks. Quality control and stress tests are incorporated in each manufacturing step, and elements and components are measured with precise instruments. Some measuring devices are laser-controlled and can detect deviations of less than 0.0001-millimeter in a lens surface or in lens centering.

CAMERA BATTERIES

Battery is one of the most important accessories of any digital camera. The quality of battery reflects that up to what extend that will support the camera. A good battery not only provides a long backup duration but also it can support the flash of the camera for more nimber of clicks.

TYPES OF BATTERIES

There are different types of **camera batteries**. The batteries differ in size, type and capacity. The most common batteries are as follows:

Alkaline Disposable Battery

Source: website of ehow (2011)

This battery is the most common and traditional. It

mainly comes in AA and AAA sizes and can be disposed. The name "alkaline" is given to the battery since it has a potassium hydroxide alkaline electrolyte. Alkaline battery is known by its name because it is based on alkaline electrolyte of potassium hydroxide, instead of acidic ammonium chloride or zinc chloride electrolyte of zinc-carbon batteries. Other battery types also use alkaline electrolytes, but normally they use different active materials for the electrodes.

Alkaline Rechargeable Battery

This type is one of the most popular recharable camera batteries and come in different sizes. Unlike other batteries these can be recharged and can retain their charge for years.

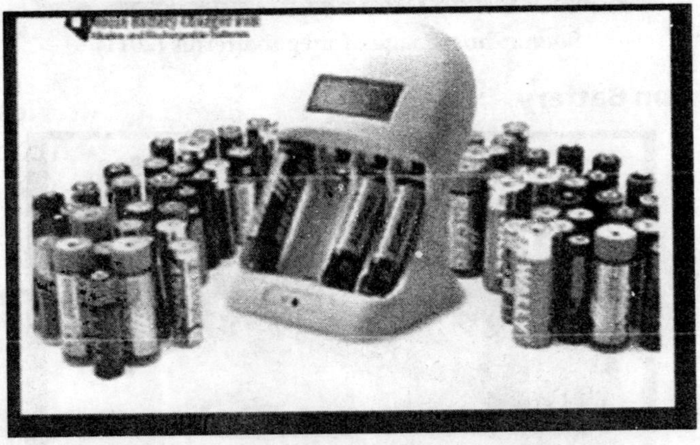

Source: **website of internetsiao (2011)**

NiCd (Nickel Cadmium) Battery

These are secondary cells developed on the alkaline chemistry with almost double energy density of lead acid batteries. This energy storage technology was invented in the year 1899. At that time nickel hydroxide Ni(OH)2 was used as positive electrode (cathode) and cadmium Cd was used as the negative electrode (anode), while alkaline potassium hydroxide KOH was taken as electrolyte. The small size and high rate of discharge capacity of these batteries made it a portable and popular tool of this industry. The sealed cove of these cells and the use of recombinant system made them capable of preventing electrolyte loss and finally it was helpful in extending the life of the battery.

Source: homepage of megabatteries (2011)

Lithium Battery

Source: homepage of ecotech (2011)

These types of batteries are used normally in our daily activities through flashlights, mobile phones, cameras and laptops etc. This type of battery is priced higher than the Alkaline AA battery and performs well even in cold weather. The lifespan of these batteries is also longer than the Alkaline AA battery and is popular in the community of photographers. However, one should ensure him/her first that the device like camera is compatible with this battery type. These battery types are most popular among all of the rechargeable battery types for portable electronic gadgets. The popularity of this type of battery is due to it's the best energy densities, no memory effect and a slow loss of charge when the gadget is not in use. Now-a-days this type of battery is achieving popularity among military and aerospace applications.

NiMH (Nickel Metal Hydride) Battery

Source: **homepage of power 2000 batteries (2011)**

Nickel Metal Hydride battery is an affordable long lasting rechargeable battery. The main downside of this type of battery is that it loses its charge when it is not in use. While using this battery it is essential recharge it before its use. NiCad and NiMH batteries are amongst the hardest batteries to charge, these batteries take more time in complete charging. While lithium ion and lead acid batteries, one can control overcharge by setting a maximum charge voltage. The nickel based battery does not has a "float charge" voltage. The charging of these batteries is based on the forcing current through the battery. The voltage to do this is not fixed in stone like it is for the other batteries. This problem makes these cells and batteries difficult to charge in parallel. Due to this vary reason one can't be assured that each cell or pack is of same resistance, and so some cells will take more current than others even when they are full. Therefore, we require a separate charging circuit for each string in a parallel pack, or balance the current in some other way.

REFERENCE

1. Edward Holmes: An Age Of Cameras (1978)
2. http://www.tlr-cameras.com/Japanese/slides/Koni-Omegaflex.html
3. http://instructables.com
4. http://sheldonbrown.com
5. http:// 3dmodelfree.com
6. http:// ehow.com
7. http:// internetsiao.com
8. http:// megabatteries.com
9. http:// ecotechninja.com
10. http:// ngureco.hubpages.com
11. http://en.wikipedia.org
12. http://answers.com
13. Introduction to digitization tools. Lia, Jua (2001)A course in digital libraries by Yerkley, A.N. and Joirgensin, C., Vol.16 no.1, pp.31-9
14. Spec Kit 214 Digitizing technology for preservation. ARL, 1996
15. Logoze, Carl & Fielding, David, (1998), Defining collections in distributed digital libraries, *D-Lib Magzine,* Nov 1998. http://www.dlib.org/dlib/ november98/lagoze/11lagoze.html (Accessed on 10/08/11)
16. Green Spun, Philip (1997). Building a Digital SLR System. Photo.net. http:/ /www.encyclopedia.com/topic/Cameras.aspx#1-1G2:2896600030-full
17. Holmes, Gillian (1996). Camera Lens: How products are made. Encyclopedia.com. (Accessed on 18/11/10)
18. Holmes, Gillian (1996). Gale's How products are made: How is a camera lens made? Answers.com.
19. http://en.wikipedia.org/wiki/Twin-lens_reflex_camera

3
Digitization Process

PROCESS OF DIGITIZATION

Now it is clear that digitization is an exciting preservation option while providing unparalleled access available to all. The technology is advancing rapidly and this raises the question of accepted standards for digital preservation technology. The standards for image capture, resolution, data transfer protocols, indexing, access, and file types must be of sincere consideration. Some of the important considerations are as follows:

Defining your requirements

The first consideration before even thinking about equipment is to define the end use of the images. On this will depend what resolution of images and what file sizes are required, and hence the equipment and time scales involved. It is also essential to consider how you will store and access the scanned images and to ensure that your budget includes the cost of the right software to meet your requirements.

Choose the right equipment

It is important to remember that scanning technology

advances quickly and enhancements are regularly incorporated into new products meaning hardware has a high depreciation rate and may quickly become obsolete and uneconomical to maintain.

The main types of capture devices available are:

SCANNERS

These are most common and traditional tool for converting print document to digital documents. A wide range and variety of scanners are available in the market, which may be choose on the basis of the features of the documents. Some of the types are:

High end A3 flatbed scanners

These are suitable for all types of photographs, transparencies, negatives and pages up to A3 size that may be laid absolutely flat. They are best used to produce files of 20 Mbyte plus. They are not suitable for bound volumes, glass plates, mounted slides, formats larger than A3 or, because they use very bright light, anything that is in danger of fading.

Source: Website of kenrockwell (2011)

Hand Scanners

A Hand scanner is a hand held manual device which is dragged on the surface of the image to be scanned. This type of scanner requires a steady hand, to avoid uneven scanning rate/speed that may produce distorted images.

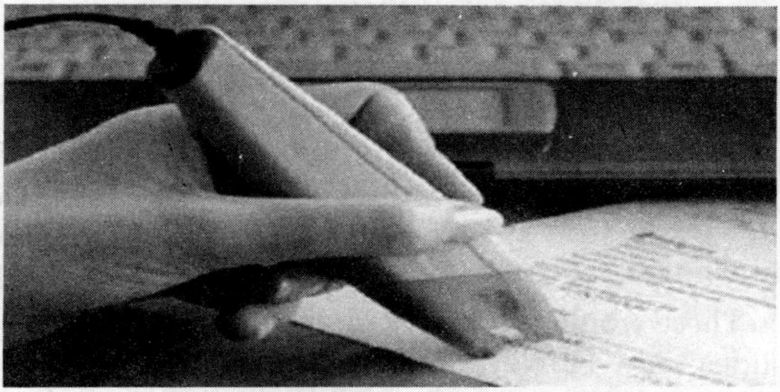

***Source*: Homepage of largescanner (2011)**

Drum Scanners

These are used by reprographic houses. Whilst they produce very high quality results they are expensive and the originals have to be fastened around a drum, which means they need to be very flexible and unmounted.

***Source*: Homepage of scanmaster (2011)**

Medium format scanning backs

Scanning backs are essentially the devices that convert a medium format conventional camera into a hi-resolution camera. With the right accessories, they are ideal for capturing items that cannot be placed on a scanner.

Pen Scanner

This type of scanner is used in the form of normal writing pen or highlighter. User is required to place the scanner on the target text and perform dragging. This type of scanner is used to scan written text.

MM scanners

These would seem to be ideal for collections made up of slides only. However, many of them are aimed at the domestic market and will not be robust enough for any reasonable sized collection. They often struggle to produce up to 18 Megabyte files of a good dpi.

Source: http:// uk.shopping.com (Accessed on 03-11-2011)

DIGITAL CAMERAS

Digital cameras come in a variety of standards. To be suitable for digitization work these must be of a professional standard and capable of 18 Megabytes plus, with interchangeable lenses and accessories

Source: **website of newdigital photography (2011)**

WORKSTATIONS

All capture devices will need a dedicated workstation of good specification and with monitors capable of proper calibration, appropriate scanning software, a CD writer and the ability to store a reasonable number of images, either on the hard drive or server.

SETYING UP A SCANNING LABORATORY

Before digitization can start there are a number of things needed to consider. Over and above the environment needed to run computers the following are essential:

- A stable power supply - fluctuations can ruin scans and make consistency impossible.
- The scanning equipment must be installed in a proper clean area - dust and dirt is exaggerated when viewed on-screen.

- The workstation must be co-located with the scanner - The person who digitize, must be able to view the scan on–screen while working.
- Check links to networks or servers are available - you will be moving large files.
- If cameras are used the ambient light should be fully controllable - overhead lighting or the variability of daylight will add a permanent color cast and make consistency impossible.
- The studio should have solid floor to prevent vibration - no digitizing is instantaneous.
- There must be sufficient room and suitable surfaces to clean items, handle and store them before, during and after scanning.
- The area must be secure.

DECISIONS ON PROCEDURES RELETING TO DIGITIZATION

Although the major part of the complete digitization process is image capturing, but being information professional, it is equally important to maintain the originality of print document, incorporate documentation based support for ensuring its easy retrieval and also to make digital document sufficient enough for achieving the best possible user satisfaction. For ensuring these issues, we should consider following things during the complete process of digitization:

Sorting and Cataloguing

Every item to be digitized must be clearly identifiable. If the digital file name is not marked or labeled on the original item, then it should carry some other unique identifier, such as an accession number, which can be associated with the file name during the scanning process.

Job Specification

Before starting the work, the rules and conventions must be decided for the job. For example:

- What file type and final size or resolution is required?
- Should monochrome prints be captured as RGB or greyscale.
- Should images to be rotated for upright orientation?
- Should operators crop to edge of item or inside edge of print/ negative? It should be specified whether captions are to be included if they are located outside the regular cropping convention, or exclude all or some types of captions.
- Should color casts to be corrected? Film transparencies and negatives very often have a color cast created by the film material, lighting conditions or processing - or a combination of all three. There are methods for detecting the presence of and correcting such irregularities.
- Is re-touching to be done? If so, to what extent, at what screen size and what is the maximum time to be spent on each item?
- Is the original unprocessed scan to be retained?
- If visible or digital watermarks are to be applied - to which resolution versions and when in the process?

Prepare your materials

Before scanning you need to prepare your equipment and originals for final handling and processing.

Batching

Where possible group original items in batches of same size/ format materials, say 100 - 150 in a batch. This will make the work easier to manage and improve productivity. It also means quality issues can be more easily isolated and corrected.

ICC Profile Checking

Ensure the monitors are all calibrated and profiled to the same standard, that the capture devices are individually profiled and that the final files are all tagged with the required device independent ICC color profile.

Pre-cleaning

If materials have been in storage for any length of time a degree of controlled cleaning may be desirable. Cleaning processes should be carried out well away from the digitization area using lint free cotton and surgical gloves.

Oil mounting

Oil mounting is a specialist technique that can significantly reduce effect of scratches, ground in dirt and other damage to negatives or transparencies.

Adjust and check your scans

This is an important step and often overlooked in the planning. Once the image is captured it must have basic checks carried out, either immediately after capture or in batches at a later time.

Color range and balance

Check that the capture device's sample range has been utilized and neither end of the tonal. If color cast correction is to be carried out, this is the time to do it.

Cropping and rotating

Carry out cropping as decided in your job specification and, if necessary, rotate the image for correct orientation.

Re-touching

Carry out re-touching to the standard decided in the job specification - this needs training and/or experience. Retouching on photographic image will always show if not done to a professional standard.

Compression

Where required create a compressed version of the image.

Multi-pack creation

Where required create screen resolution multi-pack versions.

Water-marking

Where required apply visible or digital watermarking to specified versions of the image.

Quality inspection

It is advisable for a quality inspection of say 20% of output to be carried out by a qualified person who hasn't been involved in either scanning or post-processing.

Ideal Steps of digitization

Ideally a digitization process should involve following steps:

1. Image preparation;
2. Preparation of the volumes, issues and pages of the document for scanning;
3. Scanning pages of the document;
4. Editing images of the document;
5. Using Optical Character Recognition Software (OCR) on images to edit text versions. (OCR is the process whereby a computer program "reads" the text from an image of a document and converts it into ASCII text);
6. Creating a searchable database of the text; linking text to images;
7. Mounting on Web.

Image preparation

The first step is to take all measures that are necessary to preserve the hard copy of the documents. A physical review of the document revealed much variance in the condition of the pages and that, while some could withstand scanning without any preservation, other pages would not. Consultation took place with the preservation library assistant in the rare book section at the university library and procedures were set up to follow:

1. Trim each page so that no rough edges are left;
2. Mend rips and tears with acid-free binding tape;
3. Put each issue in an acid-free envelope and store each volume in an acid-free storage box.

Important factors to consider for format

At this stage it is necessary to decide the most appropriate file format for the online version of the document. The integrity of each page had to be maintained and in order to do this, save the pages after scanning as images. There are two primary options:

1. Save the image as a PDF (Portable Document Format) file using Adobe Acrobat;
2. Save the image as a GIF (Graphical Interchange Format) or JPEG (Joint Photographic Experts Group) file.

It is investigated to save the images as JPEG files, which would be most appropriate. JPEG will allow the entire project to be uploaded as an HTML file and furthermore, JPEG retains more information as it compresses an image:

- Each page had to be kept intact so that the user could view the page online just as it appeared in the paper copy;
- User-friendliness was important. Therefore, the online version had to be searchable, had to have a minimum

of side-to-side scrolling, had to load fairly quickly and the pages had to be clear and easy to read;

- Optical Character Recognition (OCR) would work on scanned images of the document. This was a consideration as several different fonts were very small and that cannot always be recognized by OCR programs;
- With standardization the maximum number of users should be able to view it.

Scan pages of the document

Having determined the type of file to be used for the online version, several preliminary scans were conducted to determine the appropriate image type, brightness, contrast, height and width, as well as the length of time it would take for each page to be scanned. To ensure uniformity in scanning the following parameters have been investigated for set up:

Height: 12.65 in. Width: 8.18 in.

Brightness: 125 (approx.)

Contrast: 130 (approx.)

Image Type: Black and White Photo File Type: JPEG

Image Quality: 600 dpi

The selection process for identifying specific documents for digitization anticipates all the major steps/ stages of whole project implementation. The end quality of produced digital documents not only depends on the nature and importance of the original sources but also it depends on the nature and quality of the digitization process. Further it is equally important that how carefully the relevant information is captured from the original print source and later on organized, indexed, disseminated to users and finally maintained over time.

For taking a decision on to the selection of documents, these are presented in a sequence that moves from relatively abstract assessments of intellectual value to nuts-and-bolts issues concerning whether available resources and technology can provide a product that meets expectations. In practice, the pieces interact in ways that are often complex. Decisions about what to digitize must first and foremost address the intellectual value of the original sources. We are likely to be able to convert only a small percentage of existing scholarly materials to electronic form, and doing even this will require substantial investments. We therefore need to determine what it is truly worthwhile to convert. Some scholarly resources are heavily used; others are consulted infrequently. With only limited funds available for reformatting, types and levels of use can help to shape priorities.

A person reading a book, looking at a photograph, or consulting a manuscript encounters few barriers to use. One might have to handle an object carefully, or use a magnifying glass to read fine print, but in general the work is immediately approachable. The same resource, when digitized, should be equally accessible and approachable. Ideally, the electronic version will also permit new kinds of use and more sophisticated types of analysis.

Decisions to digitize must take into account the physical size, nature, and condition of source materials as they affect the characteristics of the desired product. They must likewise address whether available means of conversion can satisfy expectations for the result. Projects must also, from the very first, consider how users will be guided through the electronic version.

After an extensive analysis of the above mentioned issues it is sorted out that a librarian or an information officer should consider following points while planning for the digitization of documents in his library and information centre:

Assessment of scholarly value of Library material

Materials with marginal scholarly value are best left in their original form or made accessible in a less costly manner. Scholarly value, of course, is a subjective assessment and even the most marginal materials can support some kinds of research. Most users, nonetheless, would opt for electronic access to original monographs rather than to derivative works, or to the papers of a prominent scholar over the administrative records of a university department. Bibliographers regularly make purchase decisions that reflect their evaluation of the intellectual quality of single items or collections of materials. Similar judgments apply in choosing what to digitize.

Digitization and the intellectual value of the digital material

Scholarship can be facilitated when texts are made fully searchable by rekeying (retyping) them or by employing OCR software. Comparisons between successive drafts of a text and the final published work, for example, or with later editions and translations, are vastly simplified when the words and phrases are searchable. A concordance or thesaurus is likewise most easily mined when it is in searchable form. Electronic texts can be moved readily from one environment to another (from the World Wide Web onto the hard drive of a personal computer, and then into a word processing program, for example), shared with other users, and manipulated and reconfigured for multiple purposes. Digitized prints, drawings, and other visual resources can be viewed in groups at low resolution or inspected individually for very fine detail. Digital charts and tables, appropriately coded, can be loaded directly into statistical software packages for additional analysis.

Electronic accessibility of body of information of original books, manuscripts, photographs, or paintings

A collection of thousands of portrait images, however promising a resource, might be nearly unapproachable because of its size and the condition and dimensions of individual items. Well-indexed and in digitized form, however, the collection could be searched with relative ease for images of a particular person or for some indexed characteristic (the country from which the portrait originates, for example). Likewise, the digitization of large-format architectural drawings could enable comparisons of small- and large-scale drawings, different views of the same architectural feature, or sequential phases of construction.

Increased value of the combination or aggregation of original sources increases their value

Digitizing related scholarly monographs, like building a coherent collection of paper copies, can strengthen the context within which each title is approached. Ephemera-leaflets from a political campaign, for example-are often most useful when studied in the aggregate, as are posters, broadsides, and popular literature. Harvard has digitized daguerreotypes from thirteen repositories to facilitate the combinations and comparisons that are otherwise precluded by the fragility, value, and dispersion of the original images.

Popularity of digitized source material which is being consulted among scholars

Intensive use does not automatically make a collection a good candidate for digitizing. If the primary audience is local, for example, and if competition for a particular resource is not a problem, access may already be sufficient. Ephemera produced by a community political organization may be of great interest to local scholars and of limited value to a worldwide audience. On the other hand, if use is heavy and widespread, digitizing may at once guarantee convenient and reliable access, and make it possible for some institutions to discard their original copies. The JSTOR project, through which a large array of core scholarly journals is being made accessible in digital form, is a prime example of an initiative focusing on high-use materials.

Digitization may provide wider access

Low use may signal that a collection has marginal intellectual value, but there are many other reasons for valuable materials to have generated little interest. A collection may be held in a remote location, for example, or be owned by an institution with highly restrictive access policies. Bibliographic records may be poor, as is often the case with pamphlets. The value of digitizing such materials may go beyond the simple fact that the resulting files can be widely distributed. Broader access, as it creates a new community of users, can also facilitate more active scholarship.

Physical condition of the original materials limit their use

Some resources are too fragile to be consulted. Aging newspapers or palm-leaf manuscripts that break at the slightest flex simply cannot be browsed. In such cases, a digital copy might be provided to improve access, and a microfilm or other photographic surrogate made to ensure long-term survival. (Film can be made from a digital file or vice versa.)

Sources may also be at risk because of high user demand or extraordinary monetary value

A nation's founding documents, glass-plate negatives of vanished architectural sites, or rare maps may benefit from the creation of digital copies that satisfy the purposes of most users. These files do not necessarily need to meet archival standards. They are created to protect the originals from handling.

Related materials are so widely dispersed that they cannot be studied in context

Cooperative efforts to digitize disparate pieces of a greater whole can create or restore a more usable collection. Papyrus fragments, a prominent individual's far-flung correspondence, scattered photographs of a particular subject or by a specific photographer and broken serial runs are among the many materials whose coherence, accessibility, and scholarly utility can be enhanced through digitization.

Manageable size and format of Digital files

Digital resources need to match users' technical capabilities and equipment. Most require Internet access and standard web browsers, or a CD-ROM drive. Images delivered to the Internet in formats other than JPEG or GIF require additional software for viewing or printing. Even when electronic resources are optimized for on-screen delivery, some network connections, particularly those via modem, are still far too slow to support browsing of digital collections at satisfactory speeds. And scholars in some locations may lack training opportunities or the ongoing technical support needed to take advantage of the electronic environment. These limitations, however, are not necessarily reasons to rule out digitizing. The worldwide trend is toward greater capabilities. Moreover, the more important the resources available electronically, the greater the incentive to acquire the network, viewing, and printing technology necessary to use those resources. Digitization may, in and of itself, stimulate improved access.

Digitization and the needs of local students and scholars

Immediate demand can inject a measure of practical reality into decisions to create electronic resources. A historian may choose to teach from digitized images of manuscripts that would otherwise be unavailable to a large class. Because ready access to shared electronic files can transform the classroom, proposals to digitize in support of immediate teaching needs may garner faculty support.

Various approaches of Digitization and its facilitation to a researcher

Different digitizing techniques result in electronic files with different characteristics. These in turn can correspond well or poorly with scholarly needs. If the goal is to provide an image-based finding aid that helps users identify original materials of interest, for example, mounting slow-loading high-resolution images would be counterproductive. If, on the other hand, the intention is to reduce or eliminate handling of original materials, an image that fails to convey all critical information embodied in the original will fail to serve its intended purpose.

The simplest approach to digitizing involves use of a scanner or digital camera to create electronic pictures (bitmap images) of original materials

Decisions concerning the number of dots recorded by the scanner (resolution), how many shades of gray or colors will be recorded (bit depth), and other factors related to scanning equipment and settings will determine how well the digital product replicates the original. High-quality bitmap images can usually capture all the significant detail in texts or graphics. Scanning rare and unique texts or visual resources can make them accessible to users who would otherwise never see them. In such a case, merely reproducing the original in electronic form represents an extraordinary enhancement.

For textual materials, post-scan processing can support expanded capabilities

Scanned text can be processed with Optical Character Recognition software to produce searchable indexes. OCR software is now only occasionally employed in digitizing projects because it cannot yet interpret accurately all fonts and alphabets, and because it adds significantly to per-page costs. Text can also be rekeyed to create ASCII files-very straightforward digital text files that permit searching by keywords or phrases. In some cases this enhancement is the primary justification for digitization. Directories, dictionaries, and indexes are all significantly easier to use when specific words can be searched within a well-designed digital file.

ASCII texts accommodate key-word searching (e.g., searching for all instances of the word "temperance") and some kinds of analysis, but they do not readily replicate the structure and format of an original document. Without special coding, researchers cannot directly consult the seventh paragraph of the third chapter of a particular text. Nor can they search for all occurrences of "welcome" used as a verb rather than a noun. These capabilities become possible in marked-up texts, which are coded to highlight elements of structure, format, and syntax. The Standard Generalized Markup Language (SGML) is the emerging model. One SGML application, the Encoded Archival Description (EAD), is being used to create electronic versions of archival finding aids.

These and other approaches to digitizing carry very different costs, benefits, and resource requirements. While electronic versions can be more versatile than original materials, in some cases they hinder research. A scholar studying bookbinding or papermaking, for example, is poorly served by a reproduction of any kind. So too is the scholar whose immediate access to a large and important collection of literary works is sacrificed in order to serve a worldwide constituency-perhaps because bound volumes have been disbound for scanning.

Digitization increase the utility of the source materials

Digitization can enhance original materials in many ways. Image quality can be improved by eliminating extraneous stains and marks. Thumbnail images of visual resources (photographs, drawings, and paintings) can be browsed to discover patterns, trends, and relationships among individual items, and specific images can then be scrutinized at higher resolution. Likewise, patrons can review scanned images to identify needed materials before requesting that they be retrieved from storage.

Electronic transcriptions of texts, in ASCII format or marked-up files can be linked to bitmap images of original documents. Readers can then decide for themselves whether "authoritative" transcriptions are in fact accurate. Comparisons of different versions of a text are likewise simplified. Related texts and images can be assembled together within a single, unified corpus. Examples such as the Geet Govind project of UNDP, administered by Indira Gandhi National Centre for Arts, New Delhi is an interactive, multimedia document on Archaic and Classical India, suggest the potential of electronic texts.

Almost all electronic products will provide basic links that allow users to navigate them (to locate a particular map within a printed text, for example). The degree to which a digitization project exploits electronic links will depend upon its intended use. For digital resources created as pedagogical tools, predetermined connections are part of the package. Products intended for research tend to be less aggressive in ordaining relationships among sources, since their creators assume that researchers will build their own structures of meaning.

Critical features of the source material must be captured in the digital product

The cost and nature of digitizing hardware and software continue to evolve, and preferred solutions are likely to shift as well. It may sometimes make sense to defer certain digitizing projects so that technology can catch up to needs. The success of a project to digitize oversized maps at Columbia University, for example, depended partly on the ability of users to see detail and read place names. As a result, the maps were scanned at relatively high resolution, thereby creating challenges for digital image delivery and presentation. File sizes were very large and initially outran the capacity of the library's computers and network. Greater bandwidth and more powerful machines have enhanced functionality.

The cost and nature of digitizing hardware and software continue to evolve, and preferred solutions are likely to shift as well. It may sometimes make sense to defer certain digitizing projects so that technology can catch up to needs. The success of a project to digitize oversized maps at Columbia University, for example, depended partly on the ability of users to see detail and read place names. As a result, the maps were scanned at relatively high resolution, thereby creating challenges for digital image delivery and presentation. File sizes were very large and initially outran the capacity of the library's computers and network. Greater bandwidth and more powerful machines have enhanced functionality.

Digitization process retained source material

Automatic sheet feeders are fast and efficient, but they may destroy brittle paper. Digital cameras can minimize the manipulation of source materials, but subjecting certain media-watercolors, for example prolonged lighting is problematic.

Issues of hardware which is used for conversion

Color slides, for instance, cannot be fully represented by scanners that create only black-and-white images. Even a color scanner with limited capacity to reproduce tonalities will be inadequate when high-quality images are important. Digitizing equipment can be expensive, and the costs may be difficult to justify when use is sporadic. Some projects may thus be done most economically if they are contracted out. Agreements with external vendors, in addition to specifying technical conditions, performance expectations, and handling guidelines, must fully define ownership and distribution rights for all digital products.

Digitization of information resources which continue to grow

Ongoing commitments and extended arrangements for copyrights may be required when collections are still expanding, as is the case with current journals and annual reports, or the papers of a living individual. Consultations with scholars and other experts can be particularly useful, since the long-term value of current materials is often difficult to discern.

Users navigation within and among digital collections

Printed sources orient readers by means of tables of contents, chapters and sections, pagination, indexing, and formatting cues. Manuscript materials often rely on finding aids linked to the organization of file folders. Photographs may be mounted in albums. At a minimum, electronic products need to provide the same kind of functionality. The process may require several steps. For a multi-volume work that has been scanned page by page, for instance, each page is a separate computer file that must be individually labeled and stored. The files for critical pages of the work-for example, the title page, table of contents, and the first page of every new chapter-must then be linked to electronic navigational tools so that they can be easily located.

Existence of Digital files in the Information Centers

Bibliographic records, finding aids and indexes can all be adapted to include references to electronic resources. Nonetheless, our ability to determine what has been digitized remains well behind what we know about materials that have been microfilmed or photocopied.

One of the principal challenges is to determine what information is essential in describing an electronic product. The "Dublin Core" and other special initiatives for structuring and standardizing descriptive data propose to combine information about the technical characteristics of digital files, their location, and a summary of their contents. The resulting records are known as "metadata." Their function is to provide users with a standardized means for intellectual access to digitized materials. Despite these and other initiatives, projects to catalog digital files are only in the developmental stage. No system has yet been widely adopted for tracking the digitizing activities of libraries, although new approaches continue to emerge.

Better delivery of Digital products to users

Alternative modes of digital storage and delivery must be considered from the outset of a project. CD-ROMs, for instance, are distributed and used differently from information made accessible over the Internet. The differences are reflected in hardware requirements, software, and ease of use. CD-ROMs are sometimes bundled with software for searching and analysis that is superior to that generally provided for Internet files. On the other hand, access to CD-ROMs is limited to individual workstations or small networks, while Internet files can be made available to a very broad audience. And Internet resources, by nature, can be updated or augmented without requiring users to replace objects that have become obsolete.

Internet products, however, generate questions of their own. How immediate must access be?

Files can be mounted on a server so that they are instantaneously available on-line. They can be stored on disks in a jukebox and loaded on demand ("near-line" access), or kept off-site ("off-line") and retrieved and delivered on demand. Near-line and off-line access can save on server space and requirements, though there are countervailing staff costs associated with retrieving and mounting the files. Expected demand, file sizes, fee structures, and available staffing and equipment must all be considered.

Authorization of use of the digital resources, and required circumstances

Copyright holders may limit distribution rights, institutions may be unable or unwilling to provide the infrastructure needed to support universal access, and cost-recovery enterprises cannot by definition make their products available without restriction. Digitizing projects must thus consider access policies and control, pricing mechanisms, and billing procedures. Access issues impinge upon selection decisions in a number of ways. A university may mount high-resolution images of unique holdings for scholarly use (a medieval manuscript, an important collection of drawings), but would not allow unauthorized publication of those images. Moreover, electronic resources cost money that must be secured through subsidies or fees. When neither internal budgets nor external subventions provide adequate financial support, digitization will require a paying audience.

Access, when it is not universal, must be managed

Current alternatives include passwords, direct user

fees, and limitations according to organizational affiliation. Different capabilities for viewing, downloading, and printing may be offered at different prices or to different sets of users. There are many options, each reflecting a different pathway toward a self-sustaining endeavor.

Ensure the integrity of the digitized data

The malleability of electronic products makes them particularly useful for many kinds of scholarship. Digitized files must be embedded with detailed information concerning the methods used to create them. The same information should be included in external bibliographic or descriptive records. Users who are consulting or copying the sources must also be able to confirm that the files they see or receive match the originals. Means to authenticate and protect digital products, long available in financial and industrial applications, are only beginning to take hold in the scholarly world.

Adequacy of the existing technology infrastructure to fulfill local demands

Robust computer systems and an appropriate number of work stations are perhaps more easily provided than such ancillary features as network printing capabilities in the library and in offices, classrooms, and residences.

The Goal of the project is to long-term preservation of deteriorated materials

Preserving documentary resources in electronic format presumes that, to the greatest extent possible, all the information contained in the original material has been captured completely and accurately. This requires careful attention to significant detail, whether the smallest text characters on a page or all the shades and tones of blue and green in a seascape. Targets for resolution, grayscale, and rendition of color either exists or is being developed to ensure the needed detail and fidelity.

Digital preservation also requires a supporting organization and infrastructure dedicated to storing the electronic files and to migrating them to new formats and/ or media as technology change. Unless these capacities are all in place, digital files cannot be regarded as permanent. Creating an enduring digital preservation master file is a multidimensional task with long-term implications. Hybrid projects, in which digital files are complemented by copies on microfilm, alkaline paper, or some other stable medium, provide the insurance that exclusively electronic projects do not.

Availability of already digitized source material

As we have seen, it can be difficult to determine whether a specific item has been digitized and by what means. If an electronic copy does exist, is it accurate, satisfactorily functional, and accessible? Does it take advantage of the capabilities of current technologies? If the existing product does not serve the intended purposes of the proposed project, a new version may be warranted.

Benefited User Group of the proposed digital product

It is important to consider whether the product will support better teaching or research and enable students to learn more, or in different ways-if, for example, texts or images are more fully revealed. Digitization may allow librarians to manage collections and provide services more effectively, or to provide traditional services such as copying or interlibrary loan at lower cost or at less risk to collections.

Commensuration of the intellectual value of the proposed product with the expense

The limited resources available for digitization might have greater impact if they were directed at another project, or directed toward an entirely different approach to providing access-through exhaustive indexing perhaps, or microfilming, or some other type of reformatting that would prove in the end more useful to scholars.

Creation of acceptable digital product at lower cost

When materials are scanned to support short-term course work, for example, careful (and expensive) post-scan processing to eliminate extraneous marks and speckles or to deskew misaligned images may be a waste of time. Likewise, an adequate substitute for full-text scanning of little-used journals might be provided by linking scanned tables of contents and indexes to bibliographic records and relying on traditional forms of document delivery.

How will the proposed project address the long-term costs associated with digital files?

The accumulated body of digital products may enable savings elsewhere in the institution-for example, by reducing staff costs for reshelving bound journals, or by lowering the costs of storage, circulation, and preservation-and these savings could offset some or all of the expense of digitizing. But such savings as may be realized are difficult to predict. It is essential to realize that the costs of digitization are just beginning at the time of initial capture. The programmatic capacity to distribute and maintain electronic resources, and to migrate them to new forms as original digital platforms fail and formats and software are superseded, is fundamental to long-term efforts. In addition, there are staff costs associated with training and user support. Finally, rising user expectations may require that existing digital files be reprocessed in new ways. When OCR software is perfected, for example, unsearchable bitmap images of texts could be thought unsatisfactory. Projects that do not plan for change may become obsolete, and therefore irrelevant.

Research libraries are eagerly embracing the digital world

They are acquiring access to great quantities of electronic materials produced outside their walls. At the same time it becomes essential to maintain digital versions of all worthwhile existing text material of their own holdings. A careful review, analysis, and planning can yield electronic resources that are functional and faithful to the original sources, and that support new kinds of scholarship. A detailed plan of work, regular assessment of progress, closely documented adjustments and corrections, and the retention of other project-related data can strengthen the knowledge base for future efforts.

QUALITY ASSURANCE

While performing digitization work, It is essential that all digitization work undergoes a series of quality control analyses at each and every stage. Regardless the digitization work is done by in-house unit of the library or the assignment is outsourced. Before initiating the process we should identify the standards and specifications of various regulatory agencies/authorities. Bearing in mind limits on time and finances, some form of sampling may be necessary to reduce the costs of this process, as with the NARA who state that at a minimum 10 images or 10% of images (whichever number is higher) need to undergo quality control (these should be selected randomly from the entire collection) (Lee, 1999). Lee further mentions that the Ideally Quality Assurance (or QA) must be performed on all master images and their derivatives with each step being fully documented. The types of things one should look for are:

- size of image
- resolution of image
- file format
- image mode is correct (i.e. colour images are in colour, not greyscale)

- bit depth
- details in highlights and shadows
- tonal values
- brightness
- contrast
- sharpness
- interference
- orientation
- noise
- alignment of colour channels
- cropped and border areas, missing text, page numbers, etc.
- alignment of image (i.e. excessive skewing that is not the result of the such things as the tight binding of a book)
- missing lines or pixels
- dithering
- poor quality interpolation with access and thumbnails
- text legibility

The overall return should be checked for file name integrity, completeness of job, and overall meeting of digitization project scope. NARA recommend that if more than 1% of images looked at fail the above quality control checks then the job needs to be redone. The Library of Congress concurs with many of these findings. For the American Memory Project running under the NDLP (National Digital Library Program) it established a fifteen-point workflow practice for the Quality Review stage covering such areas:

- Verify delivery of 100 percent of files
- Inspect 10 percent of file contents
- Ensure technical requirements have been met

- Provide feedback to contractor
- Review any re-work

Aids and more specific guidelines to help in the testing of such ideas as contrasts and noise are available with accepted test cards and procedures. A good place to start to look for these is the Photographic and Imaging Manufacturer's Association/IT10 Still Picture Imaging web page has a growing list of standards.

DIGITIZATION STANDARDS

In the world of globalization of economy and resource sharing among libraries, it is imperative to follow international standards especially in a process which is going to develop a user oriented service. In an area related to information technology, any recommendations made now would most probably be redundant in a year's time with the changing capabilities of the capture devices, software, and falling prices. Therefore, before starting the process of digitization we should explore various updated guidelines of some prominent federal agencies or voluntary organizations.

Specifications

According to Lee, the specifications suggested for any digitization project will be variable for all the reasons outlined throughout this book. At the outset, however, projects should derive a set of standards which will allow full informational capture of the originals, following accepted practice in benchmarking. Having done this, there may need to be accommodations made to take account of available resources. The standards should not just specify requirements for the archival master, but should also state the parameters for the derived products:

High resolution (Archiving resolution) used for highest quality digitization (e.g. Oxford's Celtic and Medieval

Manuscript project), for archiving file format with 'full informational capture', for outputting to high-quality print and film surrogates (in the case of graphics/text documents). The distinction between preservation copies and preservation quality images should be noted.

With graphics one of the most important factors is resolution. Different resolutions are required for different purposes, with high resolution often equating to an increase in unit costs. Furthermore, the digitization industry at present is awash with various projects digitizing at different resolution levels, and there are no archival or access standards available to which everyone adheres. Take for example a picture of a map. The digitizer scans the picture in at 600 dpi (e.g. a 5" x 4" print, with the image of the map filling the whole photograph exactly). However, if the original map was in fact 25 inches across (i.e. five times the width of the picture) the 'effective dpi' would be 600/5, i.e. 120dpi. Franziska Frey notes that 'a growing consensus within the preservation community is that a number of image files must be created for every photograph to meet a range of uses' (Lee,1999).

COPYRIGHT ISSUES

There are many interdependent and interacting factors to be weighed in selecting materials to digitize. The specific choices that result from the selection process will reflect subjective judgments, any of which may change over time. Nuance assessments, ambiguity, and shades of gray are all to be expected.

Questions concerning copyright, however, are far more clear-cut. Simply stated, if a proposed digitization work involves materials in the public domain, the work can proceed. If the source materials are protected by copyright but rights are held by the institution or appropriate permissions can be secured, the work can move ahead. If permissions are not forthcoming for copyrighted sources, however, the materials cannot be reproduced. Copyright assessments thus play a defining role with regard to digitization projects.

Copyright issues in the digital environment are still very much in flux and have provoked ongoing international discussion. While the broad thrust of digital technology is toward enhanced access, diminished costs, and more versatile capabilities, it is far less clear that copyright law will likewise encourage wider use. The legal strictures applicable to a particular project will vary depending on the country in which the project is based, the country in which the source materials were produced, and prevailing international agreements. Different kinds of materials, moreover, usually pose different types of rights-management issues. The performance rights associated with musical scores, for example, or exhibition rights for films, differ from rights for nonperformance materials such as electronic journals or documentary photographs. To complicate matters, all these rights are susceptible to change over time.

Digital projects must be undertaken with a full understanding of ownership rights, which is difficult as they often are to ascertain, and with full recognition that permissions are essential to convert materials that are not in the public domain. Rights that must be negotiated with the copyright holder often entail fees. The institution hosting a project may also have policies and procedures that inform intellectual property negotiations. The legal office of most institutions can provide guidance. The Internet site IFLA: Copyright and Intellectual Property Resources is a good resource for maintaining current awareness. It includes articles, reports and white papers, discussions, and information about organizations related to copyright issues, intellectual property in general, and electronic distribution of intellectual property.

REFERENCES

http://kenrockwell.com

http://www .prepres s te ch. com/us e d _prepres s _e q ui pme nt/ howtek/ howtek_scanmaster_4500.html

http:// largescanner.net

http:// newdigitalphotographytips.com

4
Digital Library Management Suites

DIGITAL FILE MANAGEMENT SYSTEMS

DSpace

Hewlett-Packard Company (HP) awarded $1.8 million in March 2000 to MIT Libraries for an 18-month collaboration to build digital library software, DSpace, a dynamic repository for the intellectual output in digital formats of multi-disciplinary research organizations. HP Labs and MIT Libraries released the system worldwide in the year 2002, under the terms of the BSD open source license, one month after its introduction as a new service of the MIT Libraries. As an open source system, DSpace is now freely available to other institutions to run as is, or to modify and extend as they require for meeting local needs. From the outset, HP and MIT designed the system to be run by institutions other than MIT, and to support federation among its adopters, in both the technical and the social sense. (Smith, 2003)

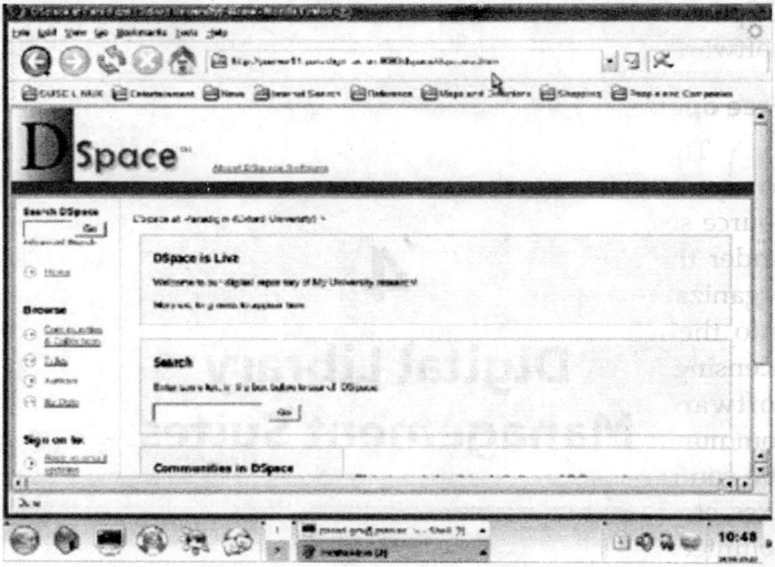

Fig. Dspace home Page

DSpace preserves and enables easy access to all types of digital information. This may include text, images, moving images and data sets. Being an open source software, it is supported by an ever-growing community of developers. This team of developers is committed for continuous expansion and improvement in the software.

WIDER ACCESSEBILITY OF DSPACE

Largest community of users and developers worldwide

DSpace has over 900 organizations that are currently using the DSpace software in a production or project environment. The most common use is by research libraries as an institutional repository, however there are many organizations using the software to host and manage subject based repositories, dataset repositories or media based repositories. A census of Institutional Repositories in the United States was done by CLIR in 2007 and found that

DSpace was the preferred Institutional Repository system software of the 446 participants in the survey.

Free open source software

The DSpace open source platform is available for free to anyone and can be downloaded from the sourceforge open source software repository. The code is currently licensed under the BSD open source license. This means that any organization can use, modify, and even integrate the code into their commercial application without paying any licensing fees. Of course, we hope if you improve upon the software, you will contribute that code back to the community for everyone's benefit. Today there are more than 100 contributors around the world contributing code, bug fixes, etc. DSpace software is managed by a smaller group of volunteer developers (called committers) that work together to plan releases and integrate new features and bug fixes submitted by the community. See our DSpace Contributor Listing for a full list of all known contributors to the platform.

Completely customizable to fit your needs

Some of the key ways you can customize the DSpace application to suit your needs are as follows:

Ability to customize or theme the user interface : You can fully customize the look and feel of your DSpace website so it will integrate seamlessly with your own institution's website and can be more intuitive for your users. DSpace provides two main user interface options: the traditional (JSP-based) interface, and Manakin (XML-based) which provides various "themes" out of the box.

Ability to customize the metadata : Dublin core is the default metadata format within the DSpace application, however you can add or change any field to customize it for you application. DSpace currently supports any non hierarchical, flat name space. However, it is possible to ingest other hierarchical metadata schemas into DSpace such as MARC and MODS. This requires using tools such as crosswalk and having some technical capability to map the transfer of data.

Standards compatible : DSpace complies with many standard protocols for access, ingest, and export. The standards DSpace supports include: OAI-PMH, OAI-ORE, SWORD, WebDAV, OpenSearch, OpenURL, RSS, ATOM

Ability to configure Browse and Search : You can decide what fields you would like to display for browsing, such as author, title, date etc. on your DSpace website. You can also select any metadata fields you would like included in the search interface. All of the text within a given item and metadata associated with the item, are indexed for full text search if desired.

Ability to use local Authentication mechanisms : DSpace comes with plugins for most university authentication methods, including: LDAP (and hierarchical LDAP), Shibboleth, X.509, IP-based. In addition, DSpace comes with its own internal authentication method, or can be configured to use multiple authentication methods at once. You can also build your own authentication plugin if you use a custom authentication mechanism.

Configurable database : You can choose either PostgreSQL or Oracle for the database where DSpace manages its metadata.

Ability to choose the default language : The DSpace web application is available in over twenty languages. So if English is not your local language, you can customize the language which DSpace uses. Youcan alsoconfigure DSpace to supportmultiple languages, so that the language your user sees is the 'preferred language' set in their web browser.

Can manage and preserve all types of digital content

The DSpace application can recognize and manage a large number of file format and mime types. Some of the most common formats currently managed within the DSpace environment are PDF, Word, JPEG, MPEG, TIFF files. It's worth noting that, although out-of-the-box DSpace only auto-recognizes common file formats, files of any format can be managed by DSpace. DSpace also provides a simple file format registry where you can register any unrecognized format, so that it can be identified in the future.

APPLICATIONS OF DSPACE

DSpace is being used by plenty of institutions in India and abroad. Some of the screenshots of LDL (Librarians Digital Library) developed by DRTC, Bangalore {https://drtc.isibang.ac.in/ (Accessed on 03-11-2011)} are:

1. End-user interface

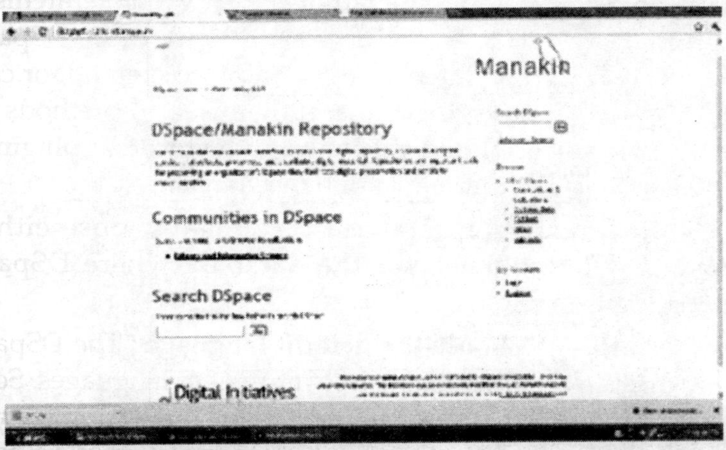

2. The user feeds his query into the search box.

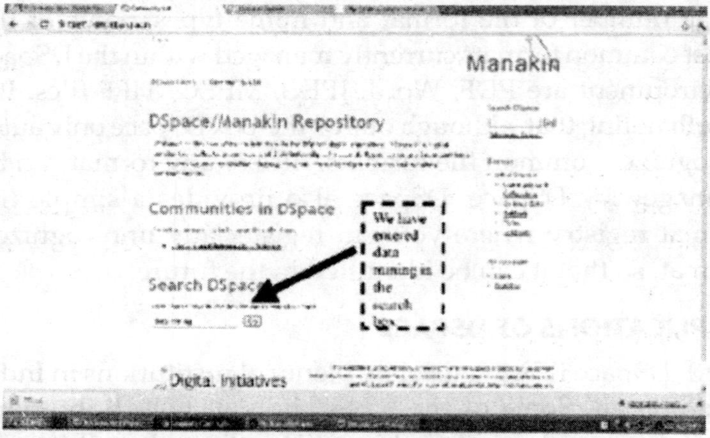

3. The output

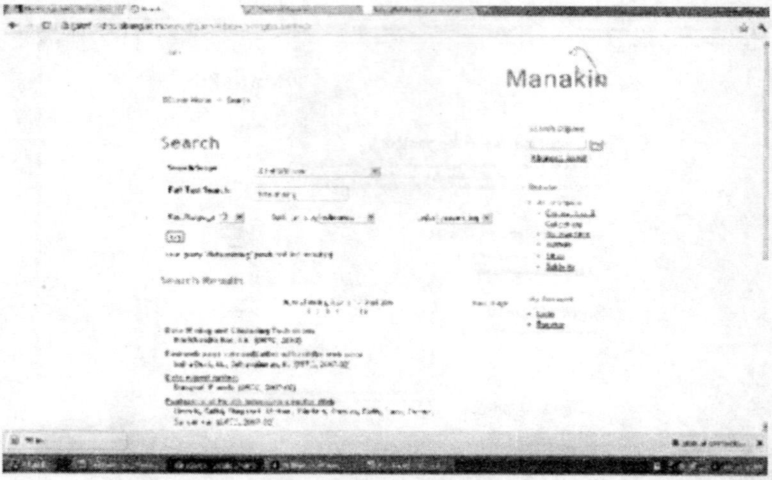

4. Out of the search results we select the document relevant to our needs.

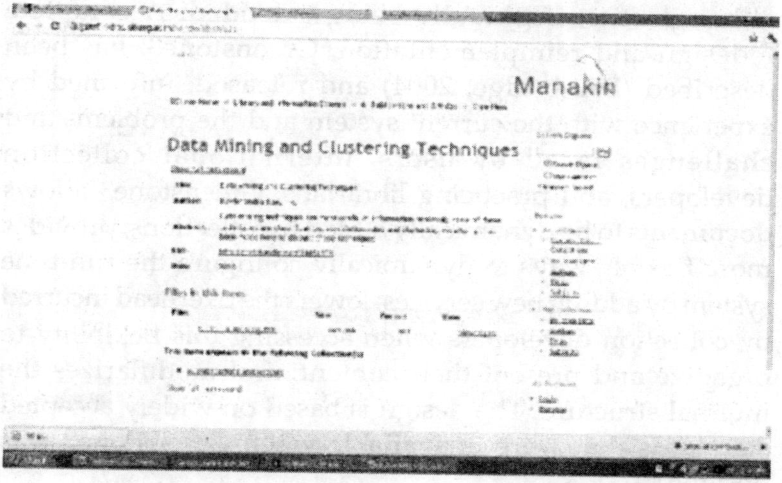

5. The document

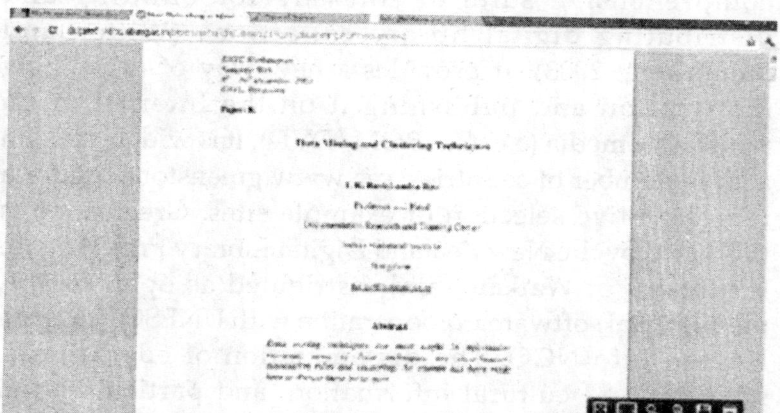

GREENSTONE DIGITAL LIBRARY

Greenstone Digital Library Software is issued under

the terms of the GNU General Public License. It originated in 1996 (Witten et al., 1996), and the current production version (Greenstone2) was designed about seven years ago, although it is continually being extended. A complete redesign and reimplementation, Greenstone3, has been described (Bainbridge, 2004) and released, informed by experience with the current system and the problems and challenges faced by users, international collection developers, and practicing librarians. Greenstone3 allows documents to be dynamically added to collections; provides more flexible ways to dynamically configure the run-time system by adding new services; lowers the overhead incurred by collection developers when accessing this flexibility to organize and present their content; and modularizes the internal structure. The design is based on widely accepted standards that were unavailable when Greenstone2 was designed.

The Greenstone digital library software is a comprehensive suite of software for building and distributing digital library collections (Witten and Bainbridge, 2003). It provides a new way of organizing information and publishing it on the Internet or on removable media (e.g. CD-ROM/DVD). It is widely used in a large number of countries: see www.greenstone.org for a representative selection of example sites. Greenstone is produced by the New Zealand Digital Library Project at the University of Waikato, and distributed as open source, multilingual software in cooperation with UNESCO and the Human Info NGO. The dissemination of educational, scientific and cultural information, and particularly its availability in developing countries, is central to UNESCO's goals, and appropriate, accessible technology such as Greenstone is seen as a vital tool in this context.

Greenstone aims to enable users, particularly in universities, libraries, and other public service institutions throughout the world, to build their own digital library collections in the fields of education, science and culture. UNESCO hopes this will encourage the effective deployment of digital libraries to share information and, where appropriate, place it in the public domain. The key points that Greenstone makes it its core business to support include: design and construction of collections; distributed on the web and/or removable media;. customized structure depending on available metadata; end-user collection-building interface for librarians; reader and librarian interfaces in many languages; and . multiplatform operation.

Functionality with Librarian's Interface

The Librarian interface supports six basic activities, which can be interleaved but are normally undertaken in this order:

- If required, download any documents from the web that need to be included in the collection. This optional step is only relevant when the collection will contain material that is sourced from the web.
- Bring documents into a collection – whether to populate a new collection or update an existing one. Metadata files may also be brought in. Users browse the computer's file space to find documents to include, and drag and drop them into place. Any documents imported from existing Greenstone collections come with existing metadata attached.
- Enrich the documents by adding metadata to them manually. Documents can be grouped into folders (it is easy to retain existing folder structures when inherited by all documents nested within them.
- Design the collection by determining its appearance and the access facility that it will support: full-text search indexes, browsing structures, the format of items on the pages that Greenstone generates, etc. This

design facility is not available at the Assistant Librarian user level.

- Build the collection using Greenstone. This work is done by the computer; users are presented with a progress bar. This is the point where Expert users might examine the output of Perl scripts, which are presented in a scrolling window, to determine if anything is going wrong.
- Pass the newly-created collection to the Greenstone digital library server for previewing. The collection is automatically installed as one of those in the user's personal digital library, and a web page is opened showing the collection's home page.

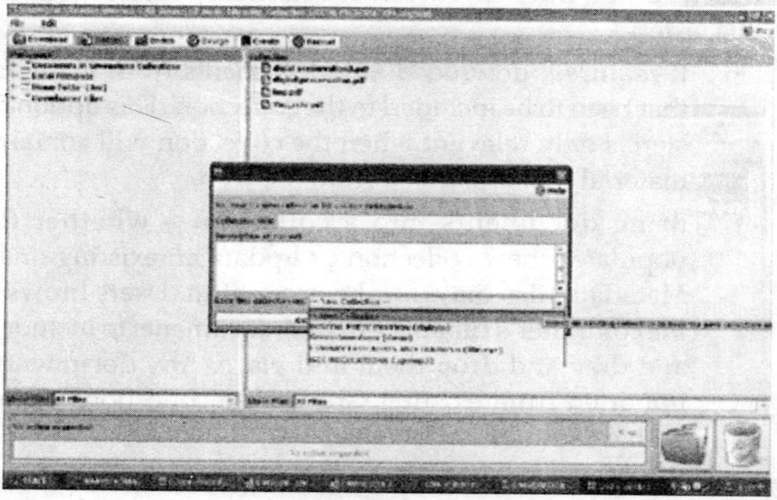

Fig. 1. Building a new collection

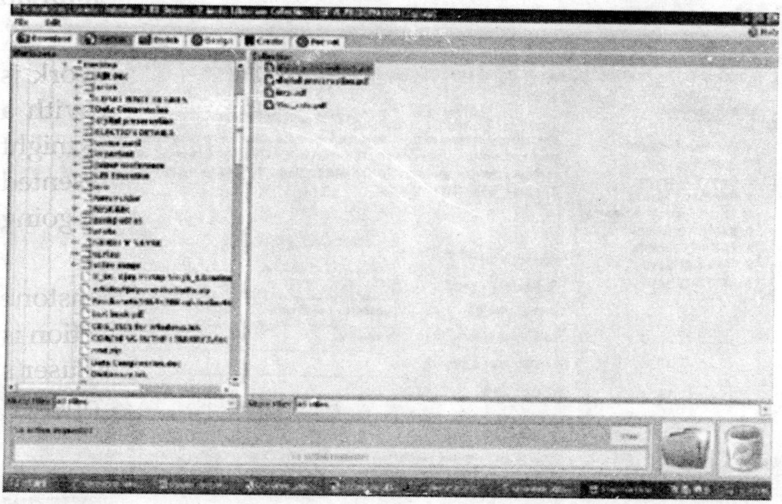

Fig. 2. Exploring the local file space

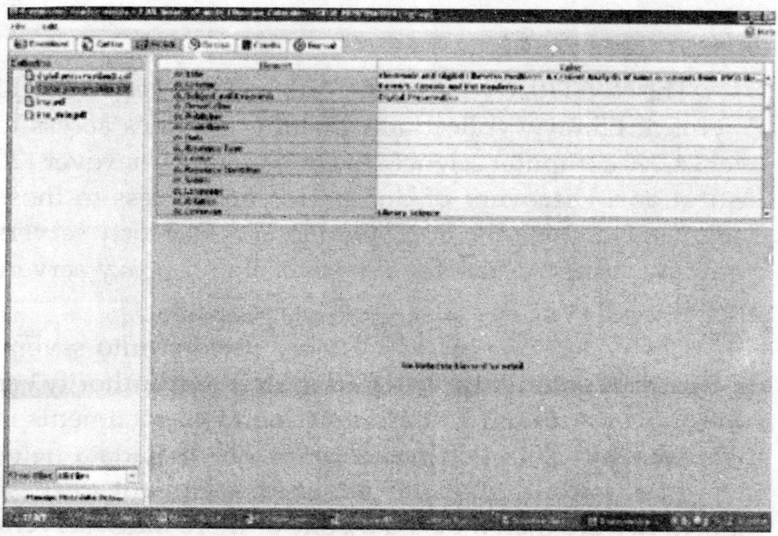

Fig. 3. Assigning metadata using the Enrich view

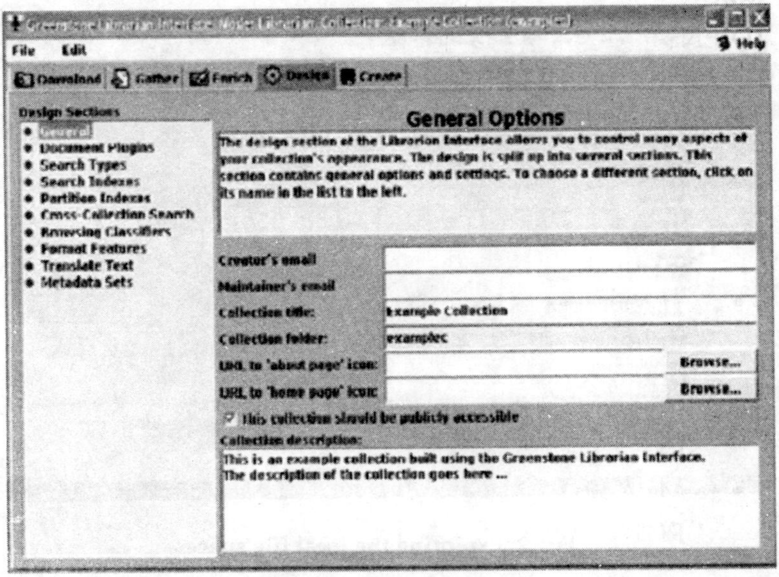

DIENST SOFTWARE

The NCSTRL (Networked Computer Science Technical Reference Library) collection currently provides access to over 24,000 computer science research reports from over 120 institutions. Discovery of documents and access to those documents involve the interoperation of over forty servers communicating via the Dienst protocol and proxy servers operating through FTP and HTTP.

The collections of NCSTRL are divided into several types of *publishing authorities*. Each publishing authority has control over addition and administration of documents in their own sub-collection repositories. The metadata fields (e.g., title, author, abstract) for each document in these repositories are then indexed by one or more index servers. The metadata is accessed through Dienst protocol requests to the respective repository. The Dienst collection service allows the federation of these index and repository servers into a single uniform collection. The Dienst protocol requests [DIENST] defined for the collection service give access to the following information:

- *The list of publishing authorities that are part of the collection.* These are the organizations and repositories that are members of NCSTRL (*e.g.*, Cornell Computer Science Department, ***D-Lib Magazine***, the CoRR artificial intelligence collection).
- *The network location*. The address and port of the Dienst index servers that store indexing information for each organization. For example, indexing information for Cornell Computer Science may be stored at foo.ncstrl.org port 80 and bar.ncstrl.org port 8083.
- *Meta information about each of the index servers.* At present, this meta-information indicates whether the index server should be considered primary or secondary. However, our intention is to expand this meta-information to include data about last update of the index and performance information that could be used for performance-based query routing.
- *The correspondence of index servers to repository servers.* This provides the index servers with information on the repository servers from which they should download meta information for indexing.

Within NCSTRL, information from the collection service is used by user interface gateways to the collection. Each user interface service is configured with the host and port number of a collection server. Periodically (every hour) each user interface gateway contacts a collection server to obtain collection information, as described above. The requesting user interface server then stores the collection information internally in a table. The user interface gateway then stores this information to later create a search interface, for example showing a list of publishing authorities from which a user may choose those to which searches should be restricted, and determine to which index servers searches should be routed.

Figure illustrates the interaction between a collection server, user interface servers, and index servers in Dienst. As shown, each user interface servers queries the collection server (via protocol) for collection information. For a specific query, an individual user interface (labeled UI_1 in the figure) uses this collection information to determine which index servers should process the query.

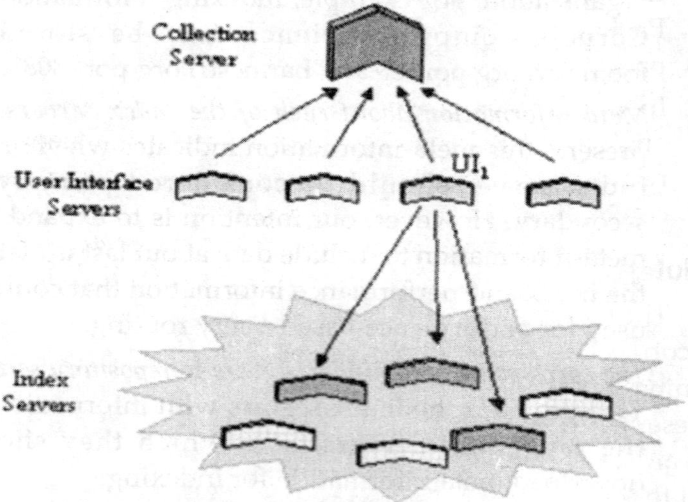

Fig. 5. Interaction between collection service and other Dienst services

The Dienst collection criteria are hard-wired into the implementation. NCSTRL collection is partitioned into sub-collections that correspond to the partitioning of the name space for documents in NCSTRL (i.e., each sub-collection corresponds to a Handle System naming authority). Second, the Dienst protocol and server implementation limits the ability of user interface servers to interact with more than one collection (and its associated set of sub-collections). This has prevented us from expanding the NCSTRL service to include additional scholarly collections; for example, physics, mathematics, etc. Finally, the Dienst architecture incorrectly conflates the functions of the user interface service with query routing. Although the collection service provides information for query routing, the actual dispatch of queries to index servers takes place in the user interface service. This limits our capacity to performing query routing that is highly collection.

- Installation of the library management service requires the ImageMagick Image Processing and Display Package and the PerlMagick Perl interface to that package.
- Installation of the index service requires a search engine able to process fielded queries and return ranked results. The Dienst implementation is configured to use freeWAIS-sf.

Modules

The Dienst software consists of a set of service modules that correspond to the services defined in the Dienst protocol. Running the Dienst server entails supporting one or more of these service modules on a server that runs in conjunction with an HTTP server. A Dienst digital library consists of a set of these services (either running on a single server/host or distributed servers/hosts) that interoperate through the Dienst protocol.

The operational semantics of each of the services are described in the protocol document. A brief description of the implementation of each service in the software distribution is as follows:

Repository : Supports the storage of digital objects in multiple formats and versions in a file system hierarchy. The set of formats available for digital objects are customizable by the administrator. Supports access to these digital objects through the verbs defined in the repository protocol. Supports the translation (either on demand or at submission time) of input document formats to other formats (using the ImageMagick library).

Library Management : Supports the submission, withdrawal, and replacement of documents from repositories.

Index : Supports the indexing of metadata harvested from distributed repositories into the freeWAIS search engine. Supports the translation of Dienst search queries into requests to the freeWAIS search engine and formatting of responses into the Dienst response format (defined by the protocol).

Query Mediator : Supports the dispatching of queries (submitted via protocol) to multiple index servers and merging of the responses from those index servers.

Collection : Supplies the information necessary for the coordination of multiple Dienst services. This information is used by Dienst services for dispatching of service requests such as query routing by query mediators to index servers and document requests from user interfaces to repositories.

Registration : Supports the storage and access of user information for authors and users of Dienst digital libraries.

Subscription : Supports the storage of and execution of persistent queries (subscriptions) on a Dienst collection.

Browsing : Supports the construction of browsing indexes and the actual browsing of those indexes on library contents.

User Interface : Provides the human friendly front-end (HTML pages) that above services.

Some of the popular libraries which are successfully using Dienst digital library software are:

- The OpenArchives Initiative.

- NCSTRL, the Networked Computer Science Technical Reference Library.
- CoRR, the Computing Research Repository.
- Cornell University Library Making of America Collection
- ETRDL, the ERCIM Technical Reference Digital Library.
- Hein online Retrospective Law Journals
- Cornell University Library Historical Math Book Collection

Application of DIENST software at Cornell University Library Historical Math Book Collection

{http://digital.library.cornell.edu/m/math/ (Accessed on 03-11-2011)}

1. End-user interface

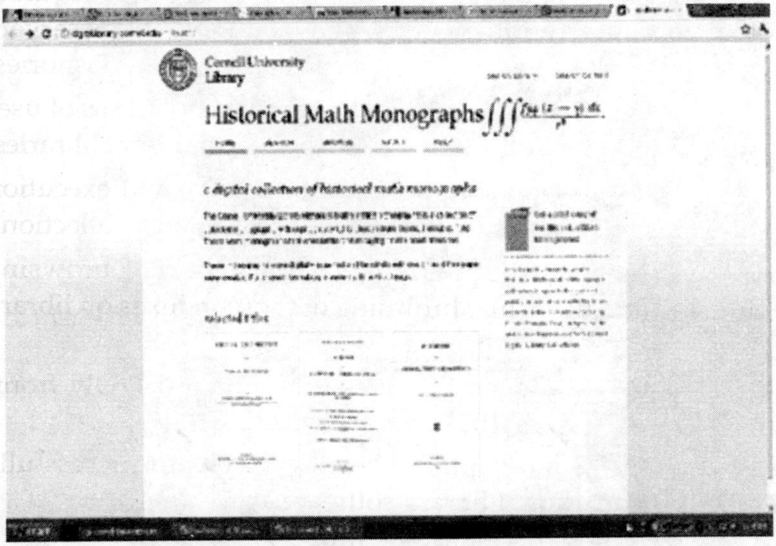

2. The user feeds his query into the search box:

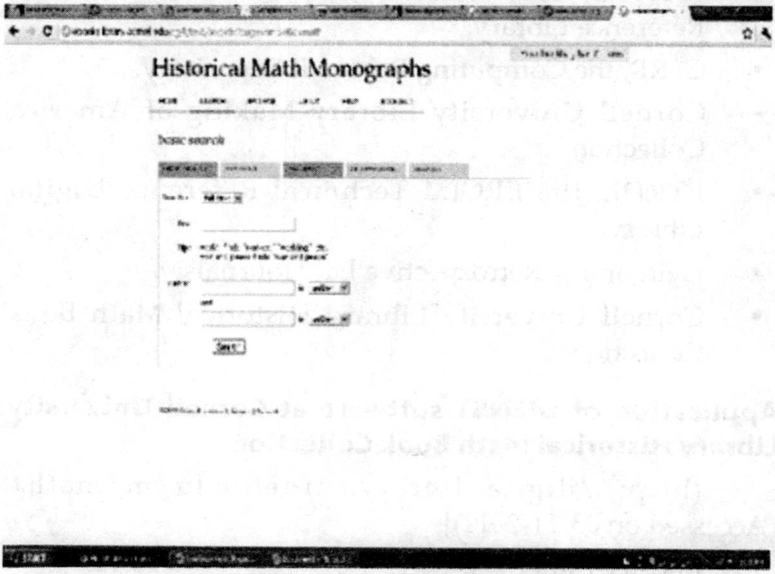

3. The output. Out of the search results we select the document relevant to our needs:

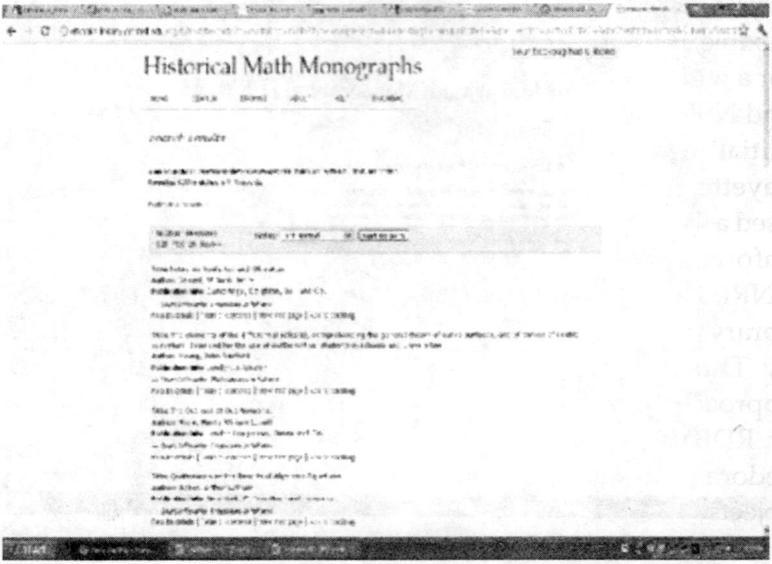

4. The document:

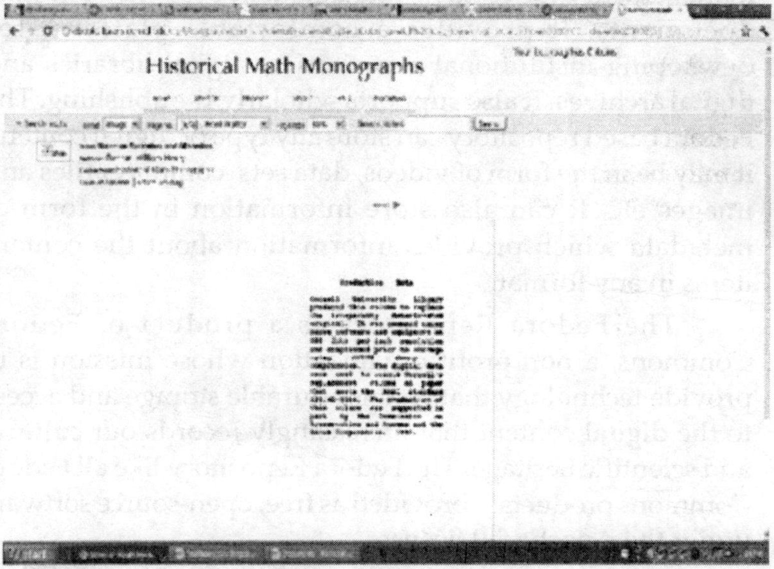

FEDORA

Fedora is an acronym for the *Flexible Extensible Digital Object Repository Architecture*. The Fedora Repository is very flexible; it is capable of serving as a digital content repository for a wide variety of uses. Fedora began in 1997 as a DARPA and NSF funded research project at Cornell University. The initial research implementation was developed by Sandra Payette, Carl Lagoze, and Naomi Dushay. Work at Cornell used a CORBA-based approach that included work on policy enforcement and extensive interoperability testing with CNRI. The first practical application of Fedora was the digital library prototype developed at University of Virginia (UVA) by Thornton Staples and Ross Wayland in 1999. The approach was redirected fit within the Web architecture and an RDBMS was added to improve performance. The UVA Fedora prototype included scalability testing for 10 million objects.

Fedora is being in use for the purpose of digital asset management and content management systems of digital documents. It provides a comfortable platform for developing institutional repositories, digital libraries and digital archives. It also supports scholarly E-publishing. The Fedora based repository can store any type of digital content, it may be in the form of videos, data sets, computer files and images etc. It can also store information in the form of metadata which provides information about the content items in any format.

The Fedora Repository is a product of Fedora Commons, a non-profit organization whose mission is to provide technology that enables durable storage and access to the digital content that increasingly records our cultural and scientific heritage. The Fedora Repository like all Fedora Commons products is provided as free, open-source software under the Apache 2.0 license.

Basic issues for the development of Fedora are as follows:

Identifiers : provision of persistent identifiers; unique names for all resources without respect for machine address.

Relationships : support for relationships between objects.

Tame Content : normalization of heterogeneous content and metadata based on an extensible object model.

Integrated Management : efficient management by repository administrators not only of the data and metadata in a repository, but also of the supporting programs, services and tools that make presentation of that data and metadata possible.

Interoperable Access : provision of interoperable access by means of a standard protocol to information about objects and for access to object content; discovery and execution of extensible service operations for digital objects.

Scalability : provision of support for >10 million objects.

Security : provision of flexible authentication and policy enforcement.

Preservation : provision to features to support longevity and archiving, including XML serialization of objects and content versioning.

Content Recon : reuse of objects including object content being present in any number of contexts within a repository; repurposing of objects allowing dynamic content transformations to fit new presentations requirements.

Self-Actualizing Objects : ability of digital objects to disseminate launch-pads or tools for end-user interaction with content.

The digital object model offers the strengths and advantages of:

- **Abstraction :** The object model is the same whether the object is data, behavior definitions, or behavior mechanism. It also does not matter what kind of data the digital objects is representing – text, images, maps, audio, video, geospatial data are all the same to Fedora.
- **Flexibility :** Implementers of Fedora can design their content models to best represent their data and the presentation requirements of their specific use case.
- **Generic :** Metadata and content are tightly linked within the digital object.

Preservation & Archiving through Fedora

Fedora's archival and preservation capabilities include:

XML : Fedora objects' XML and the schema upon which they are based are preserved at ingest, during storage, and at export.

Content Versioning : Fedora repositories offer implementers the option of versioning data objects. When a data object is versioned, the object's audit trail is updated to reflect the changes made to the object, when the change was made and by whom and a new version of the modified data is added to the object's XML. This new Datastream cascades from the original and is numbered to show the relationship between original and version. This allows users to retrieve older versions of a data object by performing a date/time search and retrieval, or the most current version if the date/time criteria are not included in the search.

Object to Object Relationships : Relationships between objects can be stored via the metadata included in the objects. This allows implementers to link together related objects into parent/child relationships.

Event History : Every object in a Fedora repository contains an audit trail, which preserves a record of every change made to the object.

A Fedora digital object consists of three parts:

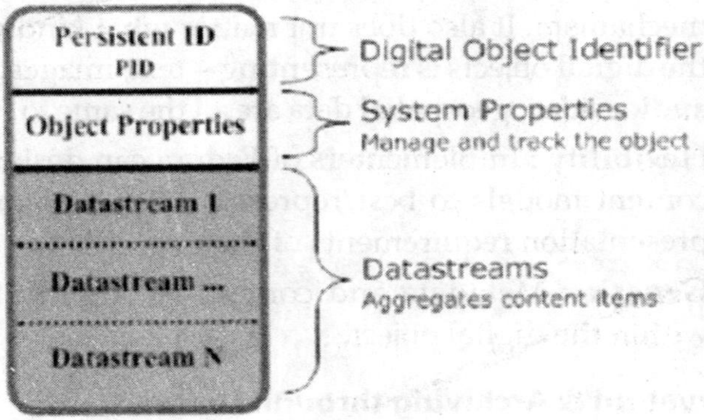

Fig. Showing the components

1. **Digital Object Identifier :** A unique, persistent identifier for the digital object.
2. **System Properties :** A set of system-defined descriptive properties that is necessary to manage and track the object in the repository.

3. **Datastream(s) :** The element in a Fedora digital object that represents a content item.

The basic properties that the Fedora object model defines for a Datastream are as follows:

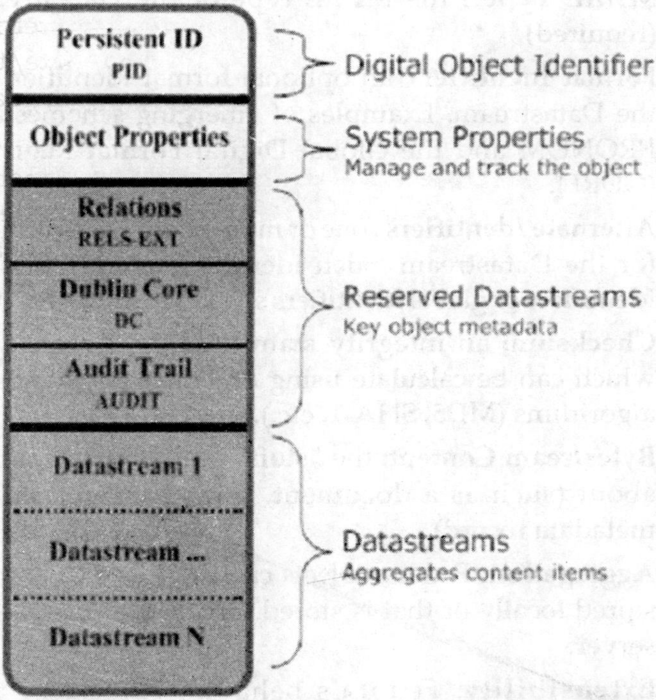

- **Datastream Identifier :** an identifier for the Datastream that is unique within the digital object (but not necessarily globally unique).
- **State :** the Datastream state of Active, Inactive, or Deleted.
- **Created Date :** the date/time that the Datastream was created (assigned by the repository service).
- **Modified Date :** the date/time that the Datastream was modified (assigned by the repository service).
- **Versionable :** an indicator (true/false) as to whether

the repository service should version the Datastream. By default the repository versions all Datastreams.

- **Label :** a descriptive label for the Datastream.
- **MIME Type :** the MIME type of the Datastream (required).
- **Format Identifier :** an optional format identifier for the Datastream. Examples of emerging schemes are PRONOM and the Global Digital Format Registry (GDRF).
- **Alternate Identifiers :** one or more alternate identifiers for the Datastream. Such identifiers could be local identifiers or global identifiers such as Handles or DOI.
- **Checksum:** an integrity stamp for the Datastream which can be calculate using one of many standard algorithms (MD5, SHA-1, etc.).
- **Bytestream Content:** the "stuff" of the Datastream is about (such as a document, digital image, video, metadata record).
- **Aggregation:** Fedora objects can refer to data that is stored locally or that is stored on any web accessible server.
- **Extensibility:** Fedora's behavior interfaces are extensible because services are directly associated with data within a Fedora object. As the services change, the objects change along with them.

Control Group

Pertaining the the bytestream content, a new Datastream can be defined as one of four types, or control groups, as follows:

Internal XML Metadata : In this case, the Datastream will be stored as XML that is actually stored inline within the digital object XML file. The user may enter text directly into the editing window or data may imported from a file by clicking Import and selecting or browsing to the location of the XML metadata file.

Managed Content : In this case, the Datastream content will be stored in the Fedora repository and the digital object XML file will store an internal identifier to that Datastream. To get content, click Import and select or browse to the file location of the import file. Once import is complete, you will see the imported file in a preview box on the screen.

External Referenced Content : In this case, the Datastream content will be stored outside of the Fedora repository, and the digital object will store a URL to that Datastream. The Datastream is "by reference" since it is not actually stored inside the Fedora repository. While the Datastream content is stored outside of the Fedora repository, at runtime, when an access request for this type of Datastream is made, the Fedora repository will use this URL to get the content from its remote location, and the Fedora repository will mediate access to the content. This means that behind the scenes, Fedora will grab the content and stream in out the the client requesting the content as if it were served up directly by Fedora. This is a good way to create digital objects that point to distributed content, but still have the repository in charge of serving it up. To create this type of Datastream, specify the URL for the Datastream content in the Location URL text box.

Redirect Referenced Content : In this case, the Datastream content is also stored outside the repository and the digital object points to its URL ("by-reference"). However, unlike the External Referenced Content scenario, the Redirect scenario signals the repository to redirect to the URL when access requests are made for this Datastream. This means that the Datastream will not be streamed through the Fedora repository when it is served up. This is beneficial when you want a digital object to have a Datastream that is stored and served up by some external service, and you want the repository to get out of the way when it comes time to serve the content up. A good example is when you want a Datastream to be content that is stored and served by a streaming media server. In such a case, you would want to pass control to the media server to actually stream the content to a client (e.g., video streaming), rather than have Fedora in the middle re-streaming the content out. To create a Redirect Datastream, specify the URL for the content in the Location text box.

Some of the applications of FEDORA digital library software are:

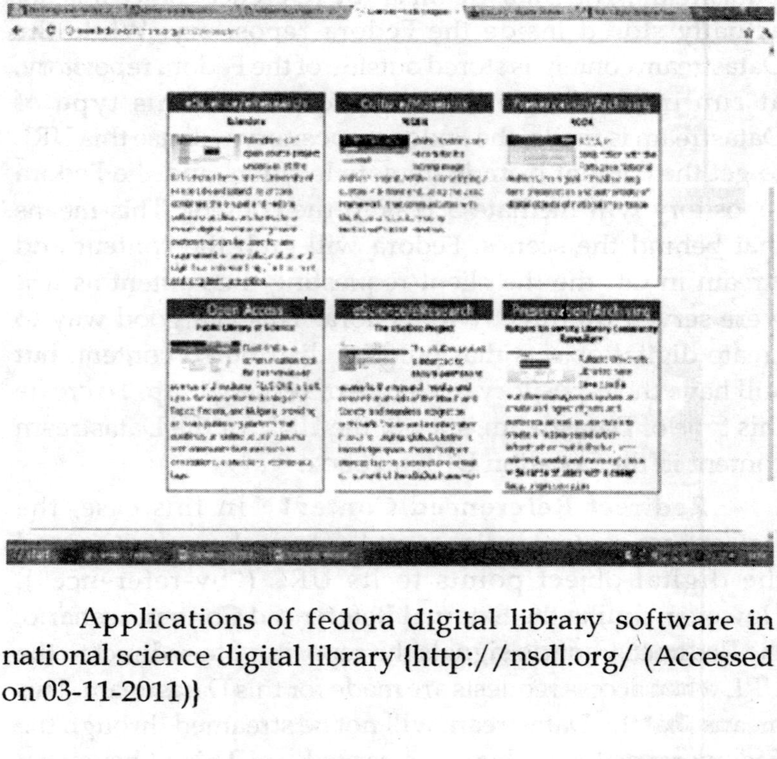

Applications of fedora digital library software in national science digital library {http://nsdl.org/ (Accessed on 03-11-2011)}

1. End-user interface:

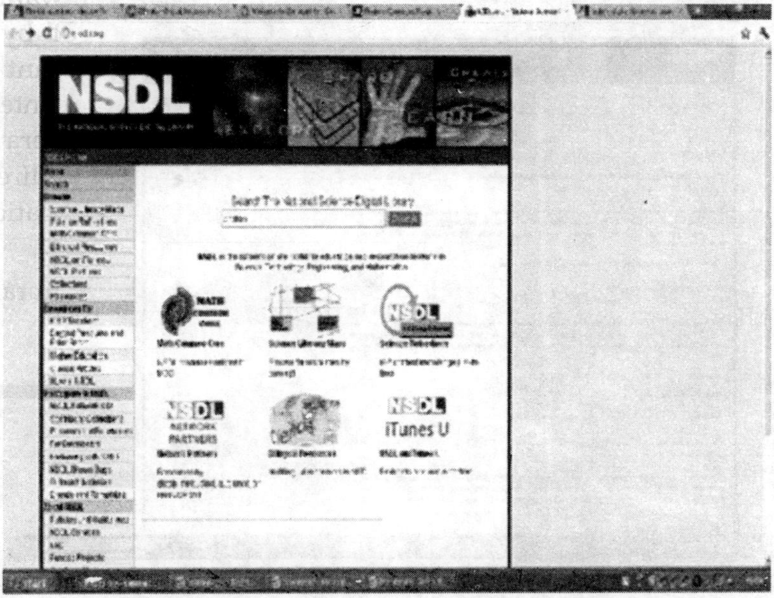

2. The user feeds his query into the search box:

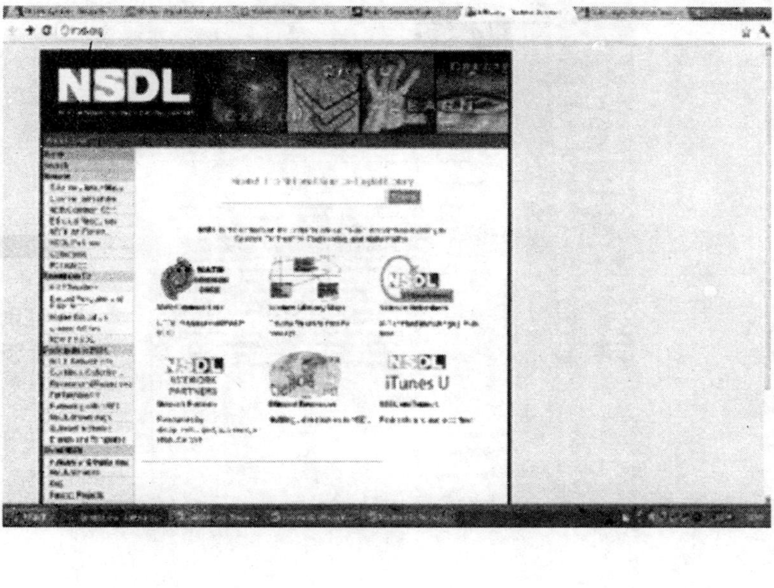

3. The output:

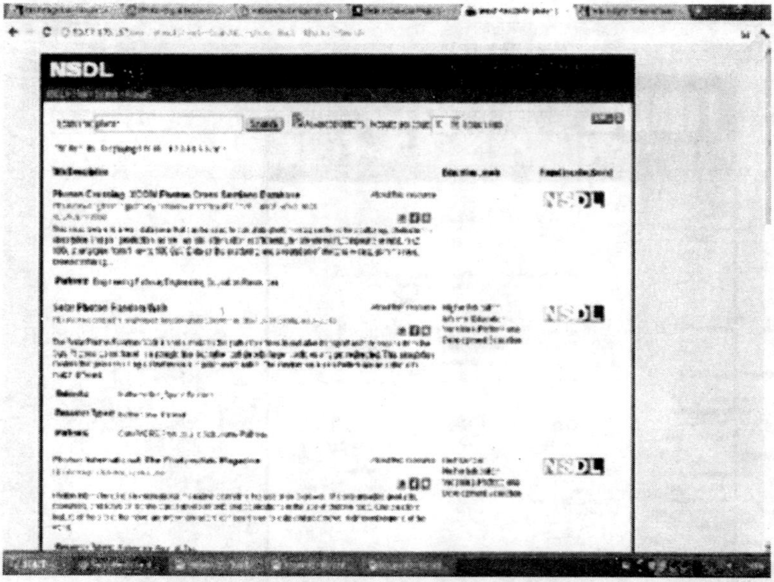

4. Out of the search results we select the document relevant to our needs:

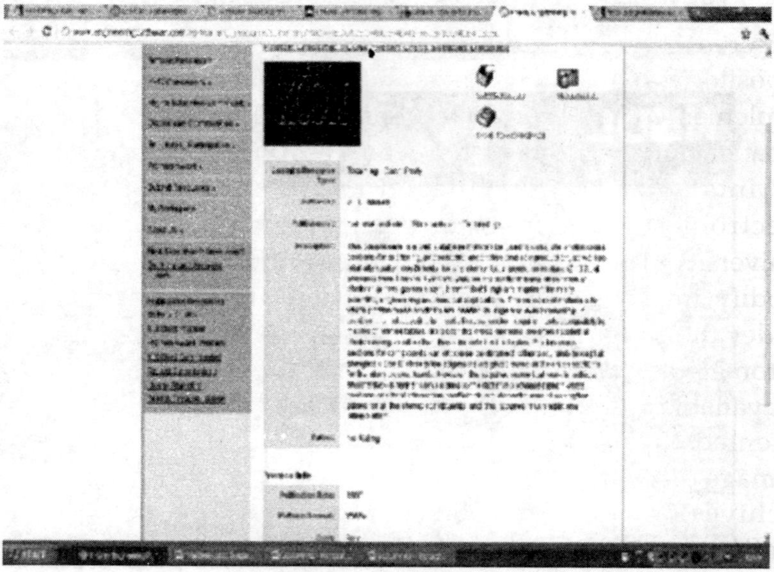

5. The document:

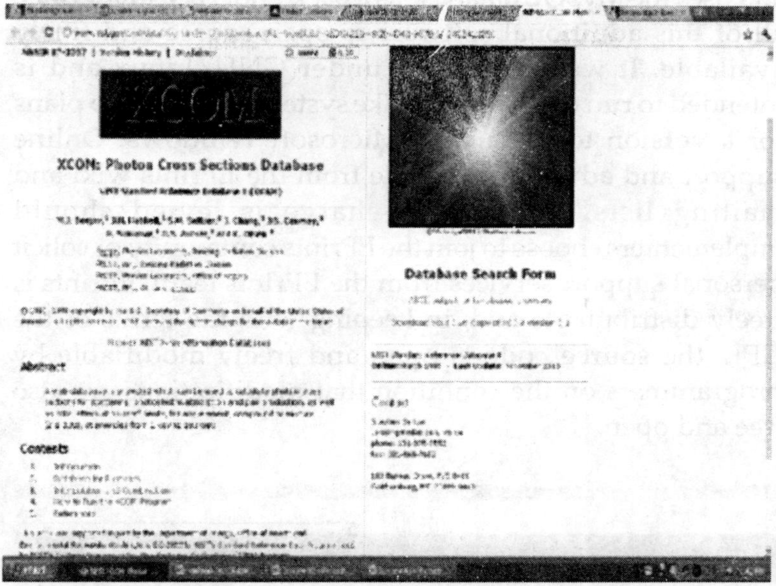

EPrints

The EPrints software package was originally designed for creating and managing open access institutional repositories of research papers and publications. It is widely implemented and is now used to store and manage a much broader range of content types and for different purposes. EPrints software is managed and developed by the Electronics and Computer Science department at the University of Southampton allows users to freely run, study, modify, improve, and release improvements of the program under the same terms. Most of the installation process is automated by way of an installation script and further help is available from the website. The default configuration is oriented towards research papers; using the system to manage different types of digital materials – such as audio archives and research data – requires changes to the configuration. EPrints is written in Perl, requires installation of the Apache web server and a number of Perl modules, and uses the MySQL database as a back-end. As with EPrints, all of this additional software is open source and freely available. It was developed under GNU/Linux and is intended to run on any UNIX-like system.There are no plans for a version to run under Microsoft Windows. Online support and advice is available from the EPrints wiki and mailing lists, although a charge is levied should implementers choose to join the EPrints community or solicit personal support services from the EPrints team. EPrints is freely distributable and, in keeping with the terms of the GPL, the source code is open and freely modifiable by programmers on the condition that modifications are also free and open.

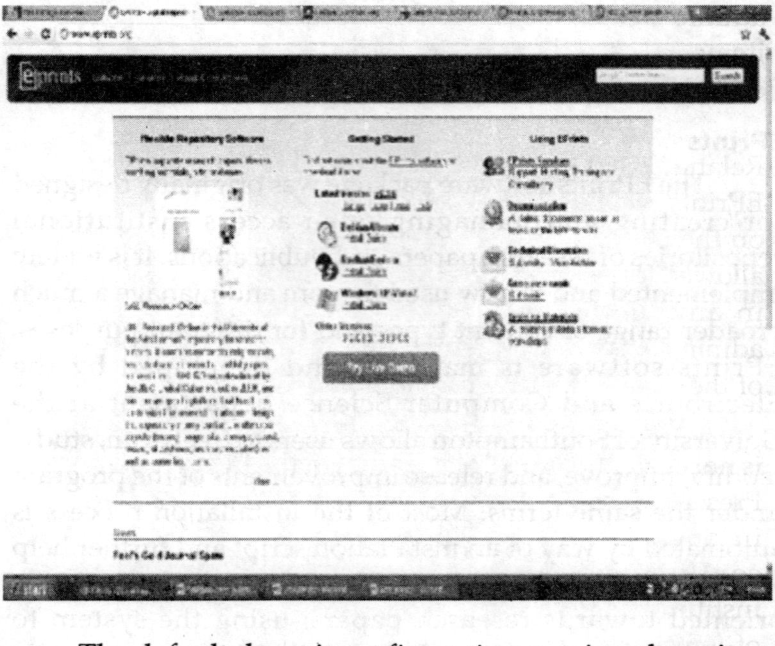

The default deposit configuration requires depositors to enter a minimum set of metadata.This set does not conform to any particular standard, although in practice, an EPrints implementation can be configured to request and store any metadata according to institutional requirements and the type of objects stored.A Dublin Core application profile for deposited ePrint items is under development as part of the JISC Digital Repositories Programme.

New objects (i.e. content file(s) + metadata) are temporarily stored in the registered user's 'workspace' until all required metadata has been entered and the object deposited: this enables depositors to put an entry 'on-hold' until all required metadata has been collected.A built-in buffer enables items to be withheld for review or approval by repository administrators before final entry into the system.This can be disabled.

Workflow : In keeping with the straightforward ingest procedures, workflow functionality is minimal. Editors and administrators can receive e-mail notification when new items are deposited and move content in and out of the submission buffer if the buffer is active.

Storage : MySQL must be installed as the back-end Relational Database Management System (RDMS) for an EPrints service. The amount of discspace required depends on the repository scale, but approximately 2MB should be allowed for each ePrint item deposited. Content can be stored in any format designed acceptable by the repository administrator during configuration. Multiple representations of the same content are acceptable.

Preservation : Functionality for long-term preservation is not currently an explicit feature of the EPrints architecture. Preservation in institutional repository software, particularly in open access, is a source of some contention, with conflicting opinions on whether it is the role of an institutional repository to undertake long-term preservation of journal and research articles that have been published elsewhere. Despite this, the EPrints team is participating in the PRESERV project to investigate and develop infrastructural digital preservation services for digital repositories.

Access : A web accessible interface enables users to search the system. Full text searching and searching on metadata fields are both possible. The software does not assume open access and can be configured to allow limited access to certain deposits or sets of deposits. The generic version of EPrints is fully interoperable with all other OAI-PMH compliant Open Archives, which means that papers in all OAI-PMH compliant Archives can be harvested using the OAI-PMH protocol.

DEMO-VERSION OF THE APLICATION OF EPRINTS DIGITAL LIBRARY SOFTWARES. {http://www.eprints.org/ (Accessed on 03-11-2011}

1. End-user interface:

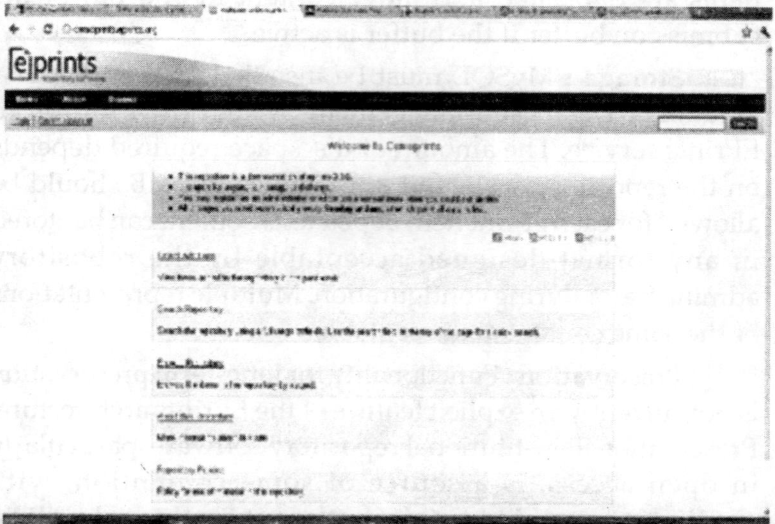

2. Select the appropriate subject from the subject directory:

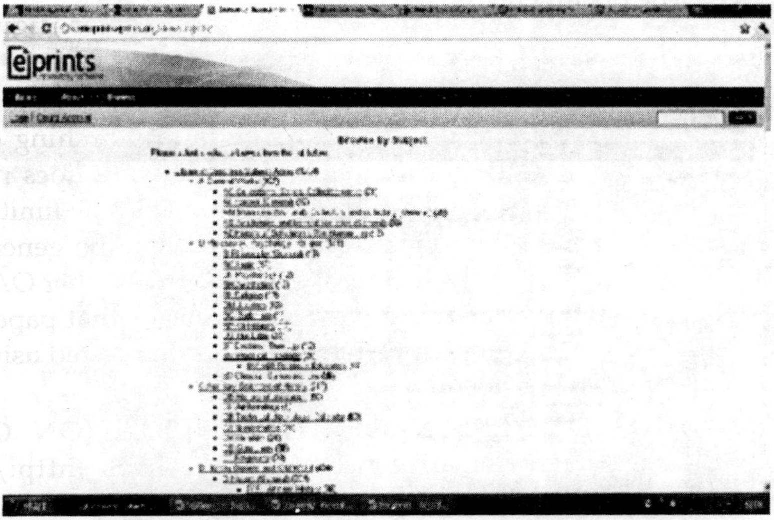

3. Documents in a chosen subject directory:

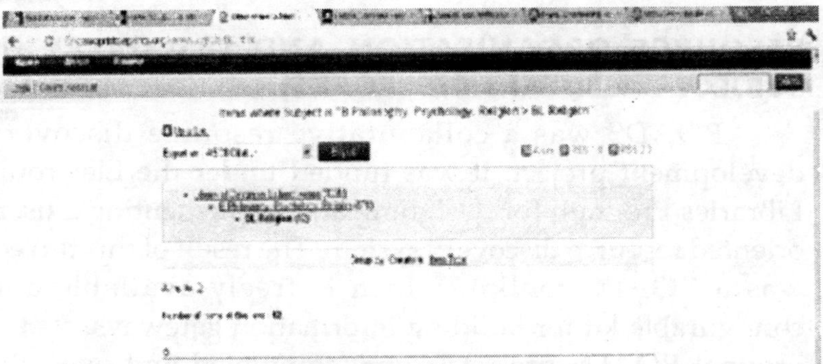

4. The document:

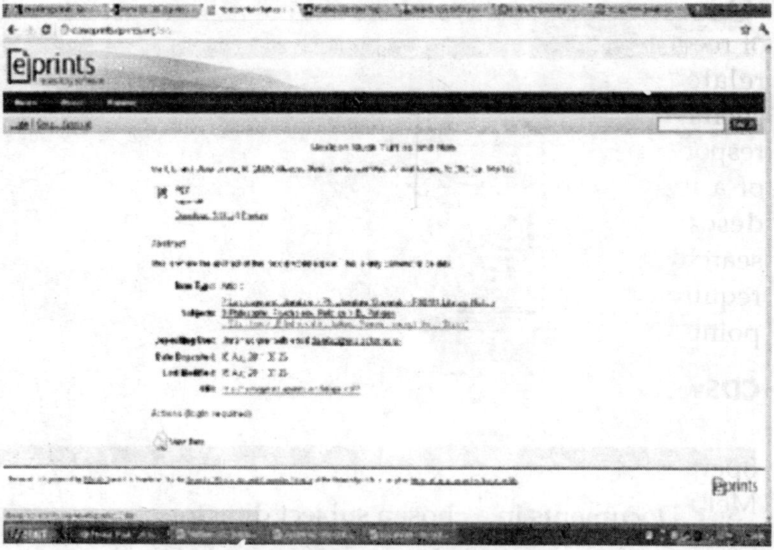

RESOURCE ORGANISATION AND DISCOVERY IN SUBJECT-BASED SERVICES (ROADS)

ROADS was a collaborative resource discovery development project. It was funded under the Electronic Libraries Program for designing and implementing a user-oriented resource discovery system. The result of this project was a ROADS toolkit, which is freely available and configurable kit for building information gateways. As the original ROADS project is now completed and over, the toolkit of this project is being maintained by an informal consortium of software developers who are having expertise in network-based resource identification, indexing and cataloguing. This is being done as an open-source software. ILRT is the centre which is expertise in the use of ROADS and is engaged in building several ROADS based services for varied clientele.

The software allows it user to establish and set up a **subject gateway**. On the backend, a web accessible database of records works and facilitates the search results. Records related to particular subject areas such as medicine, chemistry, technology etc enable the database for providing response of diversified queries. Each resource record consists of a number of fields like an identical URL, title, a brief description, related keywords. This gateway provide searching and browsing support with equal efficiency. The required resource can be searched through various access points in this gateway like sub-topic, sub-geography etc.

CDSware

CDSware is new software which at first existed and operated exclusively in CERN. Its creation began when Le Meur and Sanchez undertook the development one of the modules of the Library Operating System, ALEPH. After that, based on the material and the experience they obtained from they project, they continued their work by moving towards the creation of CDSware. More precisely, by the end of 1993, CERN initiated the first preprint server on the web. In 1996 this server evolved into "weblib" to give access to the whole CERN library, including books, electronic publications, and periodicals. In 2000 the "weblib" server became the CERN Document Server, which included more advanced characteristics, more functions and collections; it could run only on the website of CERN and became OAI compatible. From 1 August 2002 it has been distributed as a completed package under the brand CDSware, version 0.0.9, under the terms defined by GNU. The last version by the Development branch, v.0.1.2, was presented on 21 December 2003. The last version of the Stable branch, v.0.7.1, was released on 4 May 2005.

Characteristics and functions Technical options

Standards

OAI-PMH v.2.0.

CDSware is not compatible with Z39.50.

This program is freeware and supports the terms determined by GNU. These concern the free distribution of the software and not its price. Such software can be distributed free of charge, but CDSware charges for each service that might be requested. The code of the software is offered free of charge so that developers can modify it, change it or use some of parts to create new software that will be distributed for free. Hardware. Because of the variety of possible conditions within each organization, specific demands on CPU cannot be predicted. System demands will depend on the size of the collections, the number of users, the database platform, etc.

Software

1. Operating system: Linux or Solaris.
2. Programming language: Python and PHP.
3. Database: MySQL.
4. Webserver: Apache.
5. Search engine: CDSware uses its own indexing technology and a search engine designed for large data repositories.
6. Other: WML (website META language). ***Supported clients***. All HTML 4.0 or newer clients.

Staffing demands : Organizations will need UNIX systems administers and python programmers.

Administration of the repository and the system

Set-up. CDSware contains an automatic installation script that allows the system to be upgraded by later versions without eliminating modifications having to do with e-mail, supporting pages, or search pages.

Module-level Application Programming Interface (API). CDSware allows the programmers to modify the system's interoperability according to specific needs with the use of an API.

User registration

1. **Password management :** CDSware identifies multiple resources inside the system itself, users may select their own passwords (optional), CDSware offers password reminders, with a secure procedure that lets users who have forgotten their password choose a new one on their own.
2. CDSware verifies the identity of subscribed users and has other safety mechanisms. It separates authorized users who have the right to submit documents, from the rest of the system's users. It also allows the editing of user profiles.
3. CDSware restricts access according to user type, and lets the repository administrator define user access to specific content according to the level of authorization of each user (e.g. it can permit access to a repository of reports of a specific Department only by the teaching staff).
4. CDSware has multiple authentication methods that let the repository administrator define different levels of access and restrictions according to the user. Some documents might be accessible to anyone; others might be accessible to an academic community according to the IP addresses; and some others only to a restricted number of users according to their IPs/ passwords.
5. CDSware restricts access according to the level of the File/ Object. The repository administrator can restrict access to specific parts of a file.

6. CDSware manages copyright issues for documents that have been submitted to it. For each specific collection there a different copyright policy is possible. The ability to have different policies at the document level is not currently possible.

Submissions management

CDSware specifies multiple collections inside the system.

1. Those collections may be identified according to specific criteria, like subject, type of contents, aim and target group. The group of users might be academic departments, schools, etc. according to the needs of each institution. CDSware supports hierarchy within collections, as well as virtual collections (that is, it can create new virtual collections with objects from other collections).
2. CDSware defines different submission parameters for each collection. It allows the repository administrator to define different ways of submitting the documents according to their content and different review/validation parameters for each of the collections or for different user groups.
3. A special homepage for each collection can be built according to its specific needs.

Metadata

1. CDSware's basic metadata scheme is MARC21. It also supports the creation of basic Dublin Core (DC). The Open Archive Initiative (OAI) protocol additionally offers the ability to search even in non-certified DC fields (that is, additional fields not part of basic DC).
2. Since basic DC sometimes is inadequate to satisfy the needs of a specific organization, OAI supports the parallel use of metadata sets, allowing repositories to

use additional metadata specifically for each specific collection.

3. So as to be more effective, metadata harvesting from individual users can be supervised, controlled, and corrected before their final distribution to the public.
4. CDSware allows the export of metadata in OAI-MARC 21 in XML.
5. CDSware lets the system administrator prevent OAI harvesting from the repository.
6. Metadata fields may be added or deleted.
7. CDSware allows the repository administrator to predefine fixed values in metadata fields to simplify their inclusion.
8. The documents retrieved by the user appear on the first screen in their simplest and most comprehensible form in HTML format. This screen, like all the others, can be formatted and can include all possible elements and in any desirable form. Additional screens present the elements of the bibliographic records in MARC21 HTML format. Bibliographic data are saved in XML MARC, but MARC HTML provides a different and more comprehensible form for the common user.
9. Support for Unicode allows the use of almost all languages.
10. Accepted content is updated and indexed in real time.

Searching abilities

The system supports:

1. Full text searching (this refers to the internal searching of the system, the recovery software, and the presentation layer – not to third-party search engines);
2. Truncation/wildcards (* ¼ multiple characters, ¼ one character);

3. searching in all metadata fields.;
4. searching in selected metadata fields (e.g. only in the title or the author field); and
5. browsing.
6. Google and other search engines. The HTML formats used in the documents of CDSware can be created so as to permit searching through the web.

Cost

CDSware distribution is free under the terms of GNU. This not only means that there is no cost, but also that it can be modified and redistributed for free. It is a freeware, but that does not mean that CERN undertakes any official obligation to provide help for its technical support and installation. If a library or other organization requires help, it can be provided for a charge that is defined after a special agreement. Of course, there are electronic help lists and in practice there is easy and free support via e-mail or telephone, at least for initial installation problems. The copyright belongs to CERN.

SECURITY IN DIGITAL RIGHTS MANAGEMENT (DRM)

Security measures deployed in current DRM implementations. General requirements for security in DRM systems are explained first. Next an analysis of the security model in DRM is given. Then we take a look at various security technologies and solutions used for DRM. A DRM system requires persistent content protection, meaning that protection has to stay with the content. For example, a digital movie can be delivered securely over the Internet using standard cryptographic mechanisms.

But if the recipient can save and copy the content in an unrestricted form and put the digital copy onto the Internet, many people in the world can download the movie without reduction in quality. Therefore, the required security level in DRM systems goes beyond simply granting digital licenses to authorized users. More importantly, restrictions of the content usage rights have to be maintained after the content is delivered to the end user. Essential security requirements in DRM systems include data protection to protect against unauthorized interception and modification, unique identification of recipients to enable access control for the digital content, and effective tamper-resistant mechanism to process protected data and enforce content usage rights.

1. Cryptographic Mechanisms in Digital Right Management (DRM)

- Many DRM systems are built on various cryptographic solutions that have been studied and developed for many years. To summarize, the following subsections present some of the cryptographic primitives that are commonly used in DRM systems.

Symmetric and Asymmetric Encryption

To prevent illegal copying of digital content, the content is generally encrypted using a symmetric key algorithm. Most DRM providers keep their encryption process and algorithm details confidential. This is "security through obscurity" which is contrary to the basic Kerkhoff's Principle (Internet Solutions 2001). However, a number of companies have announced that they employ wellknown cryptographic algorithms for content encryption, such as InterTrust and MediaSnap (mediasnap.com) who say they use the Advanced Encryption Standard in their DRM solutions. Compared with standard implementations of cryptographic algorithms, nonstandard implementations of such algorithms are not as trustworthy, and probably, not as efficient (Stamp 2002). Asymmetric encryption is based on the usage of key pairs– public key and private key that are mathematically related so that data encrypted with one key can only be decrypted with the other key. The digital license containing the content decryption key must be encrypted using the public key of the receiver. Therefore, only the party holding the correct private key can decrypt the content key and get access to the content.

Digital Signatures and One-way Hash

In DRM systems, digital signatures are usually used for non-repudiable rights issuing. The clearinghouse should digitally sign licenses of the digital content. Therefore, the player application on the consumer's device can verify the correctness of the usage rights and keep the signature as a proof of rights purchase. One-way hash functions combined with digital signatures are used for integrity checking. For example, the clearinghouse uses its private key to sign the hash value of the encrypted content rights. Integrity verification of the license is through decrypting the signature using the public key of the clearinghouse and then comparing the hash value with a re-computed hash value.

WEB ARCHIVING

Web archiving is the process of collecting portions of the World Wide Web and ensuring the collection is preserved in an archive, such as an archive site, for future researchers, historians, and the public. Due to the massive size of the Web, web archivists typically employ web crawlers for automated collection. The largest web archiving organization based on a crawling approach is the Internet Archive which strives to maintain an archive of the entire Web. National libraries, national archives and various consortia of organizations are also involved in archiving culturally important Web content. Commercial web archiving software and services are also available to organizations who need to archive their own web content for corporate heritage, regulatory, or legal purposes.

Digital Certificates

Digital certificates are used to authenticate or verify

the identity of the parties involved in the system. In DRM systems, it is essential to use this mechanism to ensure that the packaged digital content is from the genuine authorized content distributor. The certificates of fake packaging applications should be revoked to limit the damage they can cause.

2. Individualization

Most current DRM solutions rely on unique identification of user devices. Each license is bound to a unique playback device, so the license stored in one device cannot be transferred or used by another device. To illustrate how this works, we use the example of the individualization process in Microsoft WMRM: An individualized Windows Media Player is one whose DRM component has been individualized, which is like receiving a security upgrade (Microsoft 2002b). Content providers may require their digital content to be played only on the player that has been individualized. During individualization process, Microsoft Individualization Service generates a unique DLL (Dynamic Library Link) that is bound to the client computer using its hardware ID6. Once the player has been individualized, a public/private key pair is generated. The private key is stored in the DLL file that is generated in the individualization process. The corresponding public key is used as the player's identifier when requesting a license and the clearinghouse will encrypt the license using this key. If the player is moved to another host, it will require individualization, because there is no corresponding DLL file binding to the new host. The license granted by the clearinghouse is not transferable or usable on another computer.

In the context of DRM, individualization can reduce the damage caused by system cracking, because if the DRM module on a user's computer is compromised, only that terminal is affected. However, it introduces another problem concerning the portability of rights: When the user wants to watch the movie at his friend's place or listen to the music on his portable devices (PDAs, mobile phones, portable players, etc.), he has to acquire new licenses for every device to enable content consumption. To reduce the impact of digital licensing process on the user experience, some DRM solutions allow users to back up their licenses and restore to another computer. To prevent abuse, users can only do this a fixed number of times.

3. Digital Watermarking

A digital watermark is an imperceptible signal that can be inserted into digital content for a variety of purposes, including captioning and copyright control. An important property of watermarks is robustness to common signal transformations such as file filtering and compression, and resistance to tampering (Cox and Miller 1997). In DRM systems, watermarks can be used for binding information to digital content, such as content owners, the buyer of the content and payment information. They should be recoverable by special watermark-reading software to check content copyright and determine royalty payments. Watermarks can also be used forensically to trace digital pirates. Many companies provide a web spider service that routinely searches the web and tests for digital files that have been watermarked. The purpose of this service is to detect violations of copyright for registered content owners. Once the copyright violation is detected, content owners will be notified and the infringer will be likely taken to court. Moreover, watermarks can be used for data annotation and access control. These watermarks are called annotation watermarks (Dittmann, Wohlmacher and Ackermann 2001).

Current watermarking technology is imperfect. There is no standard watermarking solution in real applications. The robustness of many watermarking systems is not very satisfactory. The majority of copyrights marking schemes in the literature are vulnerable to attacks (Petitcolas, Anderson, and Kuhn 1998). The current state of watermarking technology is such that if an attacker knows the watermarking technique, he can almost certainly mangle the watermark beyond recognition (Stamp 2002). It is possible for a hacker to remove the content usage restrictions and add additional usage rights for himself. Therefore, merely applying watermarking technologies to the DRM solution may not be secure enough to meet the commercial requirements.

4. Legal Issues

Here we will discuss on the current legal situation in the domain of DRM, focusing on the US Digital Millennium Copyright Act (DMCA), the US Security Systems Standards and Certification Act (SSSCA), the European Union Copyright Directive (EUCD) and the Australian Copyright Amendment (Digital Agenda) Act 2000.

Digital Millenium Copyright Act (DMCA)

The Digital Millennium Copyright Act (DMCA), passed in 1998, is an American law implementing the World Intellectual Property Organization (WIPO) Copyright Treaty and Performances and Phonograms Treaty (WIPO Treaties) (Harvard 2000). DRM is backed by the DMCA. Any attempt for the creation and distribution of DRM circumvention tools even for legal reasons may violate federal law under DMCA. Several legal cases attracting a much attention were:

- The arrest of Dmitry Sklyarov, a Moscow graduate student, for defeating a DRM system used in Adobe's eBook Reader (EFF 2001).
- The lawsuit threatened against a research team led by Professor Ed Felten for breaking a DRM system developed by the Secure Digital Media Initiative

(SDMI) (Greene 2001).

- The court case against 2600.org, an open source software forum, for posting a program 'DeCSS' to decrypt the content of DVDs (Stevenson 1999). Many people claim that DMCA stifles innovation and academic freedom (ACM 2001) and is a threat to open source software development. A lot of disputes are going on whether the DMCA should be altered to guarantee free speech.

Security Systems Standards and Certification Act (SSSCA)

The Security Systems Standards and Certification Act (SSSCA) is a draft bill for a US law, being developed by Senators Fritz Hollings and Ted Stevens with the assistance of the Walt Disney Company. The bill would require hardware manufactures of any digital data processing devices such as PCs, portable music players, mobile phones, digital cameras and a lot more with a microprocessor to build in DRM functionality, including copy protection, into their products. Anyone in U.S. who produces, imports or provides digital devices without built-in DRM would be breaking the law. If the bill passes, it would not only influence hardware manufacture but also concern software applications and operating systems in America. The user is no longer allowed to modify the software running on his computer or capture the digital content on the path from storage to the screen or speakers. Moreover, it would impose a heavy burden on the manufacturers as a consequence of the additional requirement of the system. Many vendors are worried that the increased prices and the complexity of the system will drive people away from new equipments with copy protection built in.

European Union Copyright Directive (EUCD)

The European Union Copyright Directive (EUCD) is a directive for implementing the WIPO treaties in the European

Union member states into national law. If the current directive were passed without modification, it would be a criminal offence to break or attempt to break the copy protection or DRM systems on digital content. The main concerns raised by the EUCD is that it could prevent teachers copying materials for their students and prohibit academic research on security issues of an operating system or a protection mechanism. In order to develop playback tools, developers would be forced to sign licenses with the creators of a format, because it is illegal for any circumvention of copyright protection mechanism. Critics argue that the EUCD is even more restrictive than US Digital Millennium Copyright Act (Leyden 2002).

Copyright Amendment (Digital Agenda) Act

In Australia, the Copyright Amendment (Digital Agenda) Act 2000 (DACA) is similar to the US Digital Millennium Copyright Act. The DACA introduces new criminal offences and civil remedies regarding the intentional removal and alteration of electronic rights management information, typically including details about the copyright owner, and terms and conditions of use of the copyright material. Manufacture, sales and dealing with unauthorized broadcast decoding devices will result in civil remedies and criminal sanctions unless such devices are for personal use. It is illegal to provide computer programs, or manufacture, sell, import or advertise devices designed to circumvent copyright protecting measures. The exceptions to this include the reproduction of computer programs to make interoperable products, to correct errors and for security testing, activities covered by libraries and archives exceptions, the use of copyright material for the Crown, and activities covered by the statutory licences for educational institutions and institutions assisting persons with a disability under Part VB of the Copyright Act.

REFERENCES

Association of Research Libraries (1995). Definition and Purpose of a Digital Library, Association of Research Libraries, Washington, DC, available at: www.ifla.org/documents/libraries/ net/art-dlib.txt

Simon, S.J. (2008). "Information architecture for digital libraries", First Monday, Vol. 13 No. 12, available at: www.firstmonday.org/htbin/ cgiwrap/bin/ojs/ index.php/fm/article/viewArticle/2183/2059

Cronies, K.S. and Henderson, P. (2002). "Electronic and digital librarian positions: a content analysis of announcements from 1990 through 2000", Journal of Academic Librarianship, Vol. 28 No. 4, pp. 232-7.

Stoffle, P. (2003). "Continuing to build the future: academic libraries and their challenges", Portal: Libraries and the Academy, Vol. 3 No. 3, pp. 363-80.

Borgman, C.L. (1999). "What are digital libraries? Competing visions", Information Processing & Management, Vol. 35, pp. 227-43.

Choi, Y. and Rasmussen, E. (2006). "What is needed to educate future digital librarians: a study of current practice and staffing patterns in academic and research libraries", D-Lib Magazine, Vol. 12 No. 9, available at: www.dlib.org/ dlib/september06/choi/ 09choi.html

Carr, R. (2004). *The Challenge of e-Science for Research Libraries*. From http:/ /www.bodley.ox.ac.uk/librarian/escience/escience.htm.

Carlson, S. (2006). Lost in a sea of science data: librarians are called in to archive huge amounts of information, but cultural and financial barriers stand in the way. *The Chronicle of Higher Education*, 52, 35.

Lawrence, B. (2005). Function creep and institutional repositories. *Bryan's Blog*. From http://home.badc.rl.ac.uk/lawrence/blog/2005/03/ 31/function_creep_and_ institutional_ repositories.

Stamp, M. (2002). Digital Rights Management: The Technology Behind the Hype. Cupertino, CA. http://home.earthlink.net/~mstamp1/ papers/DRMpaper.pdf.

Cox, I.J. and Miller, M.L. (1997). A review of watermarking and the importance of perceptual modeling. Proc. of Electronic Imaging 97, February 1997. NEC Research Institute.

Dittmann, J., Wohlmacher, P. and Ackermann, R. (2001). Conditional and User Specific Access to Services and Resources using Annotation Watermarks. Communications and Multimedia Security Issues of The New Century. pp.137-142. Ralf Steinmetz, Jana Dittman and Martin Steinebach (eds). Kluwer Academic Publishers.

Petitcolas, F.A.P., Anderson, R.J. and Kuhn, M.G. (1998). Attacks on Copyright Marking Systems. David Aucsmith, Ed., Second workshop on information hiding, in vol. 1525 of Lecture Notes in Computer Science, Portland, Oregon, USA, pp. 218-238.

Attorney-General's Department (2000). Copyright System: Copyright Amendment (Digital Agenda) Act 2000, Australia Law Online. http://law.gov.au/ publications/copyfactsheet/copyfactsheet.html.

Harvard Law School (2000). Digital Millennium Copyright Act. The Berkman Center for Internet & Society. http://eon.law.harvard.edu/openlaw/DVD/dmca/

EFF (Electronic Frontier Foundation) (2001). FBI Arrests Programmer in Las Vegas. http://www.eff.org/IP/DMCA/US_v_Elcomsoft/20010717_eff_sklyarov_ pr.html. (Accessed July 02, 2010).

Greene, T.C. (2001a). SDMI crack team launches preemptive suit. The Register, UK. http://www.heregister.co.uk/content/archive/19555.html.

Stevenson F. (1999). Cryptanalysis of Contents Scrambling System. http://www-2.cs.cmu.edu/~dst/DeCSS/FrankStevenson/analysis.html.

Leyden, J. (2002). Alan Cox attacks the European DMCA. The Register, UK. http:// www.theregister.co.uk/content/4/25088.html.

Malla, Meena (2008). Library Services for members of Indian parliament. World Library and Information Congress: 74th IFLA General Conference and Council in Quebec, Canada during 10th -14th August, 2008.

http://www.preifla2008.ca/Presentations/LibraryServicesMembers ParliamentIndia-E.pdf

Digital Library Federation (DLF) (1998). A Working definition of digital library. Web site. http://old.diglib.org/about/dldefinition.htm

Witten, Ian H. and Bainbridge, David, (2003). How to build a digital library. San Francisco: Morgan Kaufmann Publishers.

Rusbridge, Chris (2006). Tomorrow, and tomorrow, and tomorrow: poor players on the digital curation stage. Edinburgh Research Archive. The University of Edinburgh. http://www.era.lib.ed.ac.uk/bitstream/1842/2150/2/ Tomorrow%20final.pdf (Accessed on 10/02/10)

Smith, M., Barton, M., Bass, M., Branschofsky, M., McClellan, G., Stuve, D., Walker, J.H. (2003). DSpace: An Open Source Dynamic Digital Repository. *D-Lib Magazine*,9(1) http://webdoc.sub.gwdg.de/

edoc/aw/d-lib/dlib/january03/ smith/01smith.html

http://www.hullhistorycentre.org.uk/discover/pdf/D3-4-5_v10.pdf

http://gamerides.com/index.php?option=com_awiki&view= mediawiki &Itemid= 46&article=Web_archiving